Analytics

How to Win with Intelligence

John Thompson and Shawn Rogers

Technics Publications

Published by:

2 Lindsley Road
Basking Ridge, NJ 07920 USA

https://www.TechnicsPub.com

Edited by Alden Hayashi & Lauren McCafferty

First Printing 2017
Copyright © 2017 by John K. Thompson and Shawn P. Rogers

ISBN, print ed.	9781634622370
ISBN, Kindle ed.	9781634622387
ISBN, ePub ed.	9781634622394
ISBN, audio ed.	9781634622417

Library of Congress Control Number: 2017941946

This book is dedicated to my wife, Jennifer. She has gently but consistently supported the idea of me writing a book for years. She has been the greatest source of inspiration and motivation in my life. Without her unwavering dedication and focus, this book - and a number of other professional and personal achievements - would have never have come to be. Thank you for all you are and what you mean to me – everything.

John K Thompson

This book is dedicated to my wife of 26 years, Dawn, and to my children Amanda and Jack, who bring love and balance into my life every day. They have created a foundation that supports and enables everything I do. They constantly motivate me to be a better person and enable whatever professional and personal success I might have. Thank you for being there for me and supporting me through all challenges.

Shawn Rogers

Contents

Foreword by Tom Davenport

One could argue—and probably easily win the argument—that there has been more change in analytics over the past ten years than at any other time in the history of the world. For that reason alone, a book that provides a clear-eyed assessment of the state of analytics is enormously valuable. This is that book.

Think of all the changes. We've moved from an almost exclusive focus on descriptive analytics—means, percentages, bar charts, and the like—to a healthy mix of descriptive, predictive, and prescriptive analytics. These "advanced analytics" not only supply the title of this book, but represent a major change in emphasis, which is shifting to new technologies, new analytical methods, and new approaches to decision-making.

Over the last decade we've also discovered big data (for better or worse). While the term has received a lot of hype, it really is noteworthy. The volume, structure, and flow of big data does necessitate some new approaches to storing, processing, and analyzing it. I agree with the authors of this book: we are really talking about "all data" at this point, but some types of data are still easier to analyze than others.

There have also been major changes in the technology environment for analytics. We've moved from computers in data centers to computers on our desks to computers in huge racks located far away. We've moved from batch analytics on data in a warehouse to streaming analytics on data in an Internet of Things application. Unstructured data, which never fit well into warehouses, has moved into Hadoop clusters and data lakes. Analytical software has moved from proprietary packages to a mixture of open source, traditional proprietary software, and analytical "micro-services" based on open APIs.

Perhaps the most dramatic change in analytics involves the human role played in them. As the authors of this book discuss effectively in Chapter 10, we've moved from a world in which human hypotheses govern analytics to one in which many models are generated somewhat autonomously. The authors do an excellent job at letting some hot air out of the hype about cognitive technologies, but they (and I) acknowledge that big changes in analytics are coming soon in this realm. One of the greatest challenges with analytics has always been that the targeted audiences don't always end up making full use of the analytic technologies they receive. The rise of machine learning and autonomous decision-making may help to address that issue, but the use of these tools raise all sorts of new concerns as well.

All these changes have led to a great need for insight and guidance from managers and professionals who want to employ data-driven decision-making. They will find it here.

Such guidance is particularly important now because another big change in analytics is the "democratization" of analytic technologies. Analytics were restricted in the past to a relatively small group of professionals; now many business users can employ these tools, as they are much more user-friendly. Small and medium-sized businesses can also build analytics capabilities without needing to invest heavily. At the same time, large organizations have increased the scale and scope of their analytics activities and embedded them into operational processes and systems.

I've referred to this set of changes as "Analytics 3.0," after earlier eras involving "artisanal analytics" and big data in startups and online companies. Even now "Analytics 4.0" is rapidly developing, with early adopters moving to machine learning and autonomous analytics. These analytical opportunities have opened up new possibilities for business models and strategies. The disruptive potential of these ideas may be at an all-time high.

So it's time to read this book, get off the sidelines, and start playing the game. Executives who don't understand analytics will see their careers limited, and companies that don't embrace them will find themselves at a substantial competitive disadvantage. This book provides the plays, but you and your teams must execute them.

CHAPTER 1
Competitive Advantage
Stemming from Analytics

"Where is the knowledge we have lost in information?" – T.S. Eliot

While working for one of the early startups focused on business intelligence and data warehousing, I (Thompson) had the opportunity to work on the project described below. It was exciting and exhilarating; it was the first time I had a seat at the table when decisions would make or break a career or careers, and sink or accelerate the launch and subsequent fate of a new product line. Much was at stake.

Executives at a large multinational company recognized a significant market opportunity in their home country. Their understanding of the home market stemmed from a long operating history, but the firm's state-conferred monopoly status was about to end.

The market had changed. There was a national movement to work from home. As companies closed offices and asked employees to base their operations from their homes, entrepreneurship had begun to grow significantly.

The proposed offering for this national launch consisted of two services that were required for a complete solution. The executives postulated that customers would want and adopt part 1 at any price (completely price elastic), and that they wouldn't want part 2 at any price (completely price inelastic).

This theory was the product of the team leader's intuition (or "gut feel") of how the market would react to and adopt the two components of this new solution. But the team leader also knew that his historical view and intuition may be a poor guide and could potentially sink the launch, and his career prospects, at the same time.

As such, to confirm the leader's intuition, the company deployed analytics that blended a wide range of data elements. Surprisingly, the results indicated that the proposed pricing structure was actually the inverse from what the market would want and easily adopt.

After numerous discussions and meetings, the team leader made a courageous and risky decision to flip the pricing structure, following the guidance of the most recent data and the product of the analysis. The product launch was wildly successful, resulting in revenues more than 200 percent higher than what had been forecasted for the first year. The offerings went on to serve as the basis for a successful product line that continues as a market leading offering today.

In hindsight, the decisions and choices are obvious; most people who would look at the pricing structure would know that the selections made would result in the optimal outcome. At the time, though, it was a pioneering effort to analyze this type of offering and market. Our team and the sponsoring executive came together to support the correct decision and success ensued for all involved, but it wasn't obvious at the time and it was a fraught process. What we all learned is that data and analytics were paramount to the successful outcome. We as a group and as individuals went on to design and execute numerous projects after this early win. Some of the team retired soon after the project and others, like me, started a career in data and analytics. Now, twenty-eight years after that project, I still love working with data, analytics and the people who will use both to great benefit.

NEW OPPORTUNITIES

Leading-edge firms in all industries – including yours – are constantly seeking competitive advantages. Everyone has been evaluating ways in which to leverage data and analytics. Obviously, you and your team want to win in the market; we want to help you discern the shortest and most effective route to success.

Analytics can provide that path, delivering impressive results for the projects you pursue. We, the authors, have a combined 60 years of experience in the industry, having acted in roles as innovators of leading technologies, and as analysts evaluating markets, products, and companies. As such, we have a unique view of what has worked over the past 30 years – and what doesn't work. But let's not be distracted by the technology and math involved. Instead we'll focus on how to move from ideas and concepts to effective systems, empowered staff members, and actionable results. First, let's take a step back to understand where we are and how we got here.

The Essential Role of Data and Analytics

Data and analytics provide the foundation of reality, truth, and understanding of all business processes and relationships. Other sources of information and knowledge are also important, but they have their limitations. Self-reporting and anecdotal evidence, for example, are colored by the people who are providing the account of what happened. Memory is fluid and changes with time, and people have inherent biases and vested interests in specific outcomes. That's why data and analytics are the cornerstones of insight and innovation.

That said, we do not subscribe to the theory that large amounts of data will bring about the end of managerial intuition. But we do firmly believe that large amounts of data coupled with powerful, easy-to-use, automated and distributed analytics can provide a clear picture of what *did* actually happen, and provide a framework to predict what is likely to happen in the future.

Although data contains the reality of business, it is not a complete solution. The optimal environment for decision-making is one that combines experience, theory, and seasoned intuition with data and analytics.

All these things combine to provide a clear view of the past, offer a glimpse of the future, and supply important checks and balances when making strategic bets on the most probable future path. Intuition is an essential trait of great business leaders, and it should always be part of this complex equation.

A BRIEF HISTORY OF ANALYTICS

Analytics has a long history. Most people trace the current field of analytics to operational research that was blossoming in the 1950s. That research focused on process engineering, optimizing flows, and understanding engineering problems in practical settings.

In the 1980s, business intelligence and data warehousing became very popular approaches, but they focused mainly on simple reporting and historical analyses. For context, let's define a couple terms that we will be using.

Business intelligence (BI) involves the reporting and dashboard presentation of historical information to make or support decisions. Data warehousing (DW) refers to the collection, storage, and management of non-changing data elements. The elements in DW are used in a BI system to make or support business decisions. In other words, BI is a presentation layer and DW is a data storage layer.

DW and BI often (but not always) work together to provide a complete ecosystem for information management as it relates to decision support.

In our opinion, pure business intelligence doesn't represent true analytics because, although it helps explain the past, it isn't predictive. Data warehousing plays a role in analytics as a source of data, but it requires significant planning, structuring, and cost, which can be barriers to proper use.

The 1990s saw a wave of data mining companies, including Magnify and Data Mind. At that time, IBM had created the Neural Network Utility, and one of the authors had a chance to work with the tool when it was first released. Neural network research had been ongoing for decades. The work done since the

1970s led to impressive results and a rapid proliferation of different applications like IBM's.

Today, the majority of success stories relating to image processing and recognition are based on "deep learning" technologies. Deep learning is the evolution and extension of neural networks and related machine-learning technologies. Deep learning takes its name from the fact that many of the neural networks deployed have numerous layers of embedded processing between the input and output. Much advancement has been made in this type of software's ability to learn over time, resulting in impressive results in image and data processing.

But a drawback of neural networks and deep learning systems is that they are considered "black boxes." Humans can ascertain certain aspects of how the systems learn and improve, but the exact details are opaque, and there remain factors that people cannot adequately explain.

This is one of the primary reasons why companies may opt for a less effective analytical technique, like regression analysis. A regression analysis can be fully understood, while a neural network may remain obscure.

This differentiating factor can be especially important when crucial decisions are based on the output of the analytics. For that reason, government regulators may prohibit neural networks or deep learning technologies from being used in certain applications, such as whether to approve credit for consumers applying for mortgages.

In addition to advances in the analytical algorithms used, an important innovation in the field was the development of the Predictive Model Markup Language (PMML) by Robert Grossman. PMML is an industry standard that enables people to transfer, or port, predictive models produced from data mining or machine learning. Before PMML, models developed in tightly controlled development labs could not be moved into transactional environments. With the advent and spread of PMML, predictive models can now be embedded into production and transaction environments to leverage the value of those models in real time. When people receive a call regarding the possible fraudulent use of their credit cards, they might quite possibly owe their gratitude to PMML.

DATA GETS BIG

Of course, all the advanced analytics in the world wouldn't matter much without the necessary data to analyze. Indeed, since the 1950s, data itself has served as a renewable source of competitive advantage. Recently, the focus has been on "Big Data" – a convenient label used by a wide range of participants to talk about information of all sorts. The Big Data movement ushered in a view that all data is relevant for analysis, but that wasn't always the accepted truth.

Historically, analysts considered numeric data organized in columns and rows as the predominate data relevant for analytical uses. As Big Data began to enter the conversation, the dialog had to expand to include unstructured data, namely text information. Then, as the discussion broadened, multi-structured data was brought into the mix. Multi-structured data includes text, numbers, forms, log files, and all types of data that has multiple formats.

At the current time (and for the purposes of this book), Big Data includes all data: video, images, sound, numbers, text, forms, logs, telemetry, geospatial, mapping, and more. Simply put, if it can be created, stored, and analyzed, then it's part of the Big Data discussion. If data is the fuel for innovation, then these new sources of diverse data are today's high-octane, premium fuel.

DOES SIZE MATTER?

Many executives believe that more data is better than less data, which is generally true. Often, though, more data does not lead to increased insight. According to Tom Hill, Executive Director, Advanced Analytics and Innovation, Statistica, an increasing amount of raw data does not necessarily increase the information quotient contained in the data.[1] That is, although it's certainly true that large amounts of data *can* be analyzed, it's not necessarily true that large amounts of data immediately lead to value and insight.

On the contrary, it's often the case that small amounts of fast-moving data are more valuable than large amounts of data – *if* analytics can be applied to that data in real time. Often decisions are most valuable if they can be made in real time. The value of many decisions and actions degrade as time passes or as latency is added into the process; a couple examples are detecting fraud and personalizing recommendations. Furthermore, the ability to bring disparate data together into a new and unique ensemble can frequently create the greatest value.

The underlying philosophy of Big Data is the polar opposite of traditional data warehousing. Data warehousing is predicated on carefully curated, analyzed, structured, and indexed data. Only data that is cleaned and structured can be loaded into a data warehouse.

The approach employed with Big Data is the complete opposite. In building "data lakes" and other Big Data environments, the guiding view is to obtain all relevant (or, in some cases, simply *all)* data and store it. The prevailing view is that a wide range of value is inherent in the data, and the appropriate analytics can be developed over time. In the current Big Data environment, all of the planning, structuring, and cost associated with data warehousing may actually be a detriment to delivering insights via analytics.

THE CHALLENGE OF DATA MANAGEMENT

We can't talk about analytics without discussing the challenges of data management, which are both pervasive and persistent. You may have heard the widely-quoted statistic that 80 percent of analytic effort is devoted to data acquisition and management. In many areas, such figures are akin to urban myths; in this case, it's all too true.

Earlier, we contrasted the management approach of data warehousing with that of Big Data. The former is based on the careful curating and structuring of data before it's loaded, while the latter is oriented toward obtaining and loading all relevant data. Business professionals often find it frustrating that all the work and expense put into building and maintaining a data warehouse doesn't preclude more work. For instance, if additional data sources are included in the analysis phase, or if the previous data management regimen was executed for a specific domain (the customer, for example) but then the analysis needs to be rebuilt for a different domain (the product), even more data management is required.

Another important factor in the discussion of data management is that advanced analytics relies mainly on algorithms to produce a wide range of outcomes. Each of those algorithms requires the input data to be in a requisite format or sequence. For example, in a data warehouse the data is structured as what is commonly referred to as a sparse matrix. Think of a spreadsheet with lots of empty cells. However, for the majority (if not all) of advanced analytics techniques, all cells need a value. Hence the data structures in the majority of data warehouses are not useful for advanced analytics.

It's also important to remember that these algorithms require that the data be prepared or pretreated for common conditions such as outliers, skewed data, invariances, missing values, and such. Typically speaking, most of this data management is executed just prior to the analysis on the combined input dataset. As such, the data management is well-aligned with the philosophy of Big Data: load the data now and defer structuring or additional cleaning until just before the analysis. This approach avoids the burden of dual data management, incurs the least cost, enables the greatest flexibility, and produces the most relevant and accurate results.

"ANALYTICS" DEFINED

As of late, the word "analytics" has been stretched and applied to many areas. For our purposes, we describe analytics as a continuum having the following three characteristics. Presented in order of increasing complexity and sophistication:

- **Descriptive** – These are analytics that provide descriptions of data and phenomena represented by the data. People are generally familiar with descriptive analytics: averages, distributions, clusters, categories, and so on.

- **Predictive** – These are analytics that predict what could happen given certain conditions. The algorithms review past cases and learn, or they create examples that can be compared to current datasets to obtain a prediction of the probability of what might be (or will be) happening. These algorithms, which are less familiar to laypeople, include machine learning, artificial intelligence, neural networks, cognitive computing, and so on.

- **Prescriptive** – These are analytics that take sets of predictions from ensembles of models and evaluate them for the best fit when compared with the data that describes the current environment. These systems prescribe the best results to be used in decision-making. Virtually unknown to laypeople, the technology is commonly referred to as optimization systems and cognitive computing.

As mentioned earlier, we do not consider historical reporting to be analytic. In our view, "dashboarding," reporting, and visual analytics do not represent true analytics. Instead they are variants of business intelligence, and they should be viewed as such.

On a societal level, humans tend to think about innovation or progress in terms of the ends of a spectrum. Movies, for example, tend to focus on the apocalyptic possibilities of analytics. Artificial intelligence (AI) has certainly gotten a wide range of treatments, eliciting strong reactions (think of Terminator and SkyNet).

The analytics systems being conceived of today, however, are much more in line with augmenting human capabilities (think of Watson for diagnostic support for doctors). In other words, analytics is a *tool* to support human intelligence and decision-making, and it's rare today that an analytical system would be designed as the ultimate automated environment. The current analytical systems play supporting or secondary roles to the ultimate decision-maker or subject matter expert, who would use the systems as an input when determining how best to proceed in solving a problem.

AN INFLECTION POINT: THREE MAJOR TRENDS

As far as we've come with respect to analytics, we are still in the early days of the technology. Yes, the field has existed for decades, but it has been a practice of specialists that have been removed from day to day business operations and mainstream strategic decisions. This separation is ironic because the field began as operations research and was initially dedicated to being a core part of building a company's business operations.

Most technological innovations, though, start as specialist movements. Many are built into turnkey solutions that combine hardware and software to solve a specific problem. In effect, the first databases were like appliances. Think of such an early database as a refrigerator; everything that you need is in one package. The package arrives, you plug it in, and it is ready to go. Once the software becomes refined and improved, though, the specialist hardware is jettisoned and the software runs on commodity hardware.

Analytics is no different, but the road from hardware appliance to a user-friendly interface and experience has been long. To be honest, analytics has been the purview of backroom specialists, and many of them have been all too happy with the arcane interfaces and steep learning curves. These have served as barriers to entry, resulting in higher salaries for those already entrenched in the field. Analytics vendors have been complicit in this trend, too. Analytics software has been difficult to learn, hard to use, and expensive, and the legacy vendors have liked it that way.

Recently, though, we have reached an inflection point; business leaders like yourself have come to realize that a significant competitive advantage can be gained by including advanced analytics as part of your business processes and operations. Underlying this inflection point are three major trends:

THE RISE OF "CITIZEN DATA SCIENTISTS"

As companies have begun to realize the power of data analytics, they have turned to specialized teams to investigate various options for implementing such solutions and systems. But businesses are now facing a shortage of people with the necessary know-how, as analytics professionals (that is, data scientists) have become difficult to find and expensive to retain. This has led to the rise of "citizen data scientists.

These individuals can perform many of the tasks that a data scientist can do, but they typically have less experience and lack the formal education in the field of analytics and related areas like data management or data preparation. Even so, many are sophisticated, fearless users of the technology, and their numbers are growing. At many companies, they are the ones who are driving the use of data analytics.

THE AVAILABILITY OF EASY-TO-USE, CHEAPER TECHNOLOGY

How, though, can citizen data scientists close the skills gap? One way is to provide them with software and tools that augment their abilities. These tools should execute the necessary repetitive and mundane tasks, without requiring high-level expertise. New vendors are providing software that includes "guard rails" to keep citizen data scientists from making mistakes that could compromise the integrity of the output. These new tools provide automation and improved user interfaces, which in turn help citizen data scientists be productive in their new roles.

Vendors are also enabling analytics professionals to create templates and building blocks that can be published to a corporate library. From there, a wider audience can then use these verified and certified elements to build new analytical workflows, without the involvement from a data science team.

In addition, this technology has become cheaper. In the past, only large corporations could afford the necessary tools to perform advanced analytics. Today, medium- and small-sized businesses have access. In fact, much of the software is open source. For example, a very popular application for distributed storage and processing of very large datasets is Hadoop, an open-source framework that is widely available.

THE ABUNDANCE OF DATA

In the past, companies relied on single sources of disparate relational data. These sources were generally not well-integrated, and required a level of administration and maintenance that many companies could not support. Data as a resource used to be scarce in the sense that only well-organized data was easy to use and store.

Today, data is both abundant and ubiquitous. Your company has a wide range of internal data from your factory floor, supply chain, demand chain, customers, transactions, products, merchandising, discounting, pricing, partners, competitors, and so on. In addition, you have many external sources of data available to enrich your analytics. This might include syndicated data providers like Nielsen and IRI, the U.S. and foreign governments, crowdsourced applications, and numerous third parties like Factual, 23andme, Altisource, and others. These sources will only grow as the Internet of Things (IoT) and Big Data become increasing prominent in the business environment.

Furthermore, storing and processing data have become relatively inexpensive. Of course, computers, computing services, and commercial software aren't free, but compared to past levels of required investments the cost of entry has dropped dramatically.

To summarize, in the past we were constrained by the considerable amount of data management required to build and maintain data warehouses, as well as the lack of skilled professionals to do that work. Now we have massive amounts of varied data, lower costs, and minimal barriers to entry for building large (and growing) Big Data environments.

CHALLENGES AHEAD

Although many of these barriers have fallen, the challenges that will still be faced by executives are numerous. For one thing, smart, proactive, and engaged employees are difficult to find and challenging to retain, and that's especially evident when it comes to talented analytics professionals. These professionals are now finding it more lucrative, flexible, and rewarding to act as free agents, selling their abilities in the open market. It is predicted that in just three years, the United States may be short 1.5 million managers and analysts who know how to analyze data and how to make effective decisions.[i]

One appropriate solution is to create valuable technologies and systems using *external* teams and resources, rather than attempting to hire and retain these specialized individuals as part of your staff. Indeed, a growing ecosystem is developing in which independent analytics professionals can build, market, and sell their intellectual property on a global basis.

The objective is to build analytical environments that meld into the fabric of a company's operations. People who use these systems shouldn't think, "I am going to sit down and do some loyalty analytics." Instead they should be completely focused on driving customer loyalty to the highest level possible, knowing that the analytical systems are part of the daily process. These systems should be as seamless as flipping on a light switch: nobody really thinks about what's happening in the background, but they expect the light to turn on. Analytics should be the same. It should be embedded as a seamless part of the systems that people have and use in their daily work. The best systems will be invisible.

In this book, we explain how you can view and understand data analytics. We will also provide a framework to help you determine where your team should invest to exploit the most valuable opportunities. Please note that this book isn't about the old enterprise resource planning (ERP) paradigm, in which everyone buys the same system and rebuilds their processes into the same mold as everyone else. Instead, what we're talking about is the ability to buy strategic assets and build them into unique and valuable systems, ultimately to take advantage of market opportunities before your competitors do.

CONCLUSION

Companies are changing their views of data. Rather than carefully analyzing, structuring, integrating, and storing precious little data (or large amounts of a single source of data) in massively expensive systems, businesses are now capturing data quickly, storing it, and determining how to use that information at the time of capture.

Meanwhile, data management is no longer all about the building of monolithic data stores good only for the backward-facing, predetermined-use cases. The focus is now on creating multi-part databases that can be tailored to suit the analysis performed at the current moment.

At the same time, analytics has been evolving for many decades and has now reached an inflection point in terms of tools and software. We have reached a time when each company can have its own data and analytics capability to build competitive advantage from the raw materials it possesses. In other words, now is the time to jump into the analytics game!

Endnotes:

[1] Dr. Tom Hill, Executive Director of Analytics, Dell Software Group, Statistica. 2015-2017.

CHAPTER 2
Understanding Advanced Analytics

"When the facts change, I change my mind. What do you do, sir?" – John Maynard Keynes

Post-surgical complications are a huge issue. In fact, they are the most common reason for unplanned readmissions to the hospital.[1] Now, though, the University of Iowa Hospitals and Clinics has developed an analytics system that can predict which patients are at greater risks for suffering an infection from a surgical wound.

The system uses a variety of data, including details of the surgery itself (such as the patient's vital signs, including blood pressure and heart rate) as well as information from the person's medical records (whether, for example, he or she has diabetes or hypertension). By analyzing that data, the system can predict in real time who's more likely to develop an infection. For patients who are at higher risk, doctors can then use a different technique in treating the wound or prescribe certain medications.

The results of this sophisticated analytics have been impressive, with the rate of infections for patients following colon surgery plummeting by more than 50 percent over a two-year period.[1]

ADVANCED ANALYTICS: THEN AND NOW

Advanced analytics has become an increasingly important part of not just healthcare but numerous other fields. But what exactly is this technology, and how did it evolve? We define advanced analytics as the practical use of mathematical approaches – formulas, rules, laws, and so on – to either describe the world we work and live in, or to predict phenomena that we would like to understand more clearly.

Another category of analytics are *rules-based systems*, which have been widely used for many decades and continue to be deployed in numerous business applications. In many cases, they were the best mechanisms for capturing and codifying knowledge so that that information could be managed as part of a system. Rules-based applications are very good for codifying things that never change, such as the laws of physics.

Currently, though, companies want systems that learn and evolve based on recent behavior, and rules-based systems are not the best for such purposes. Instead, the better alternatives are learning-based systems like those based on *artificial intelligence* (AI), *machine learning* (ML), and other algorithms that can be refreshed with new models based on recent behavior.

In an AI-based system, the system's recommendations move and adapt as customers' behaviors change. In the past, for example, an automaker might (or might not) have noticed that customers who bought red cars typically purchased the sport performance option. Now, though, an advanced analytics model can automatically detect this pattern and tell dealers to up- or cross-sell the performance option when a customer expresses interest in a red car. A further refresh of the model might then have revealed something else: people who are buying blue vehicles are buying hybrid models. The red car up-sell is still valid and hasn't changed, but now dealers have an additional new up- or cross-sell offer.

In addition to advances in the analytical algorithms used, an important innovation in the field was the development of the *Predictive Model Markup Language (PMML)* by Robert Grossman. PMML is an industry standard that enables people to transfer, or *port*, predictive models produced from data mining or machine learning.

Before PMML, models developed in tightly controlled labs could not be moved into transactional environments. With the advent and spread of PMML, predictive models can now be embedded into production and transaction environments to leverage the value of those models in real time. When people receive a call regarding the possible fraudulent use of their credit cards, they might quite possibly owe their gratitude to PMML.

Lastly, we can't discuss the topic of advanced analytics without talking about *cognitive computing, autonomic computing,* and *prescriptive computing,* which are all names for the same or very similar systems. In these systems, large amounts of information – for example, all the digitized medical journals in the world – are made available to a wide range of analytical methods. Given the various questions, queries, and inputs presented, the cognitive system first chooses which analytical methods to deploy. After that processing is completed, the various result sets are returned and then evaluated against the analytical objective that was set during the formulation of the inquiry (for instance, find the most relevant diagnoses for this set of symptoms). The cognitive system then presents the best-fit answer and all the other relevant results.

One of the advantages of cognitive systems is that they can interrogate vast amounts of data to find an answer (or set of answers) that no human could possibly formulate. In almost all industries today, cognitive systems are augmenting what humans can do.

In many cases, they are doing nothing more than scanning massive amounts of information to find relevant references, and then presenting them in ranked order to human experts. As cognitive systems continue to evolve, the answers they present will improve; in the near future they may generate more innovative possibilities, enabling human experts to consider an increasingly wider range of solutions.

As mentioned earlier, "cognitive computing," "autonomic computing," and "prescriptive computing" are commonly used labels for these types of systems. Over the years, IBM has invested considerable resources in the advanced analytics market, and the company's advertising has tried to ensure that the IBM name becomes tightly coupled with cognitive computing — so much so that some might assume that "cognitive computing" is actually a brand or product family of IBM. That may ultimately be the result, but right now there are still many other firms offering cognitive solutions.

THE POWER OF AGILE METHODOLOGIES

In Chapter 1, we discussed the differences between a *data warehousing* approach to data cleansing and structuring and a *big data* approach of obtaining and loading all relevant data. The latter is much more suited to agile methodologies.

These big data approaches are widely used in teams that produce output in any number of highly flexible and interactive environments. We've seen teams producing creative concepts for advertising using agile methodologies. We've also seen agile practices and concepts deployed across various business functions, including sales, human resources, and finance. And, of course, people can't seem to talk about software development without mentioning agile sprints and epochs.

As it turns out, the agile methodology also fits exceptionally well into the process of producing advanced analytics models. The previous mode of developing models took weeks, months, and even years to take a model from concept to production. That's why the process had always been in the domain of the specialists, which meant lots of job security for those individuals. No one in management understood what these teams were doing. Precious few people could vet the progress of the teams, and even fewer could evaluate whether the work produced was of the relevance and quality promised.

Today, using an agile methodology and mindset, we have moved the majority of the data management and preparation to the phase immediately before an analysis is run. This cuts down on cycle time, delays, and wasted work spent building datasets that are never used.

We have also made the focus of the model(s) much tighter. We are no longer trying to predict massive shifts in markets.

Instead, we are trying to understand much more granular events, such as the optimal time for a company to make an offer to its best customers. In certain cases, cycle times for data preparation and model building can still be measured in weeks to months, but in most instances, they are more on the order of hours and days.

Agile and iterative – that's what companies are looking for today. In some cases, businesses are looking to build, test, validate, and deploy models into production in the span of hours. If those models do not perform as expected, they are pulled out to make room for new ones. The bottom line is that speed has become of paramount importance in many markets, and companies now have access to the people, data, and tools to capitalize on potential opportunities before their competitors do.

ADVANCED ANALYTICS TODAY

Thanks to advanced analytics, we can understand customers, markets, competition, weather, and a wide range of natural and manmade environments, conditions, and situations. We can use historical data to characterize and understand patterns inherent in past behaviors and situations. We can use characterizations, rules, and understanding to build models from algorithms and formulas. We can embed these in systems to recognize the precursors to behaviors or actions that we want to forestall, lessen, or eliminate – or that we want to amplify, encourage, or extend.

Of the many advanced analytics applications available today, the commonly used includes the following:

- Recommending next actions (such as next purchases for online retailers)

- Recognizing images (for example, for security and surveillance systems)

- Real-time scoring of large volumes of streaming data (such as for financial services firms)

- Optimizing operating parameters (in factories, power plants, and other automated environments)

- Operating automated vehicles (such as self-driving cars, trains, ships, and factory trolleys)

These environments require well-defined computing architectures with significant computational horsepower. When discussing analytics in these environments, few would be surprised that advanced models are involved.

That said, people are actually more aware of the widespread use of advanced analytics than they might realize. Consumers who visit Netflix, Amazon, and many other retail websites are well-acquainted with sophisticated recommendation systems: if you liked this product, then you'll probably enjoy these other items as well. Such applications are probably the most widespread use of advanced analytics today, but that's just the tip of the proverbial iceberg. Today, sophisticated analytics is being deployed in a wide variety of fields, often popping up in the most unlikely places.

Such applications notwithstanding, advanced analytics does not provide a "silver bullet" for everything. The applications are based on data management and math, not magic. We can look at huge amounts of data, combining many different datasets, and we can apply a wide range of algorithms and models, but in the end, we ourselves must know what we seek to improve, to lessen, or to stop.

Advanced analytics can't tell us what to do, how to do it, or when to do it. That's all up to us to decide. Moreover, we can't model situations in which we lack good data. If we can't adequately describe or understand a problem or situation, then it will be very difficult (if not impossible) to build a model of it.

Lastly, we can never achieve 100 percent certainty in our models, because for that we would need to know all the possible inputs, outputs, and outcomes beforehand.

THE PROCESS OF ADVANCED ANALYTICS

There are three general stages of the advanced analytics process: model building, scoring, and maintenance. The following is a brief summary of each of those steps.

Once a company has determined the business objective of the project, the **model building** process begins. This is where the analytics team examines the data, determines which analytical techniques are appropriate, and then begins the iterative process of creating new models.

Typically, the models are built, tested, and improved through iterative cycles. Once the model is performing at a level at which the analytical team and the business team are happy with the results, the process is ready to move to the next step.

We're often asked how long the model-building process typically takes. That's an excellent question that's unfortunately very difficult to answer. In the past, the process could take years to get a model to the point at which it's ready for production use. Today, models can be built and verified in a matter of hours. So, the answer is somewhere between hours and years.

Once the models have been tested and ready, they are put into production to score or evaluate information in production systems. To clarify, scoring or evaluating information through a model typically produces a result that can be used for decision processing. A result can be a fraud score or an upsell recommendation or recognition of an image. In the scoring process, the models process transactions, data streams, groups of data, images, sounds, and more. Some of the best systems have models embedded; the users aren't even aware of the operational or decision-based improvements made by the models.

Take, for example, today's credit risk systems, which for the most part have predictive models embedded in the process flow. Credit risk analysts regularly rely on the information presented in their dashboards, but they rarely (if ever) question the models that provide the granular and accurate information used in making credit decisions.

Power plants are another example, with models that ingest streaming data about flame shape, temperature, and other environmental factors of the furnaces in operation. Using that information, the models continually provide feedback to control the systems that adjust fuel and air flow in order to maintain maximum operating efficiency.

Models always require maintenance. Models are monitored as they're operating, and it's common for them to degrade in effectiveness over time. Once a model has degraded to a specified level, it's replaced by a new version.

Models can degrade for various reasons. Most predictive models are built and trained using real transactional data or data that is representative of the state of the information that is widely available. Over time, the behavior, transactions, data, and context can change, causing "drift" in the model's performance.

As such, models need to be regularly retrained using more current information. Think of it as bringing the model into alignment with the "new normal." For certain environments, the new normal can change on a daily basis, and therefore the models operating in those conditions need to be refreshed almost every day. Other environments change on a much slower timescale, and in some cases, it can be years before a model needs to be refreshed.

Whatever the case, all models need to be monitored and refreshed at some point, and the timing will depend on many factors that your analytical team will understand and manage.

Typically speaking, analytical teams work to build the next version of a model as soon as the latest update is put into production. This cycle of model building, scoring, and refreshing continues for as long as the operational system is in use and the models continue to contribute to better business outcomes.

THE FUTURE OF ADVANCED ANALYTICS

We are still in the early stages of advanced analytics. The elements of these systems have been under construction for decades, and now with the availability of ubiquitous data, cheap computing power, high-speed connectivity, and compelling user interfaces, the age of advanced analytics is about to flourish.

Consider, for example, the growing impact of the Internet of Things (IoT): small devices connected to the Internet with the ability to communicate data about the environment that they are in and the elements that they are monitoring. Think of the explosion of data as more and more devices become connected, not just cars and equipment but also healthcare monitoring devices, household appliances, clothing, and so on.

These devices, or "things," are the end points in a network. One step up in the network is the IoT gateways: small, special-purpose computers that collect signals and information from the things. Each gateway, which may collect signals and data from up to 1,000 things, has computing power, resources, and an IP address. Businesses can deliver advanced analytics models to these gateways, which can then be used to perform a wide range of functions like the ones discussed earlier. Models on those gateways could, for example, screen data and send back only certain signals, such as those indicating failures, a degradation of performance, rates of change above the norm, or many other conditions of varying levels of complexity.

Given the level of innovation that we see today and what we can accurately foresee in the near future, we can confidently say that businesses will be able to deliver advanced analytics models anywhere in the world where a device has enough resources to store and execute the model's functions. There are no limits – cars, trains, boats, factories, retail stores, traffic lights, anemometers, thermostats, and beyond. You name it, and it will be able to receive and run an advanced analytics model. So, where is all this leading to?

People have asked when we might be reaching the end of our journey in analytics. Our feeling is this: given that analytics is merely the practical application of math to business, research, and societal problems, we will never be finished. There will always be more to do, and there will be newer and cleverer approaches to data and math, and in this sense, we will never be finished.

Our journey in data warehousing, information management, and analytics began more than three decades ago. Having been in the industry for that amount of time, we are often asked about the future of advanced analytics. Reflecting back on our experience, expertise, and the evolution of the market, we offer the following view.

It has taken 50 years to completely automate transactional systems. It has also taken about 50 years to build out the first layer of information management systems, and we have not completed that ecosystem yet.

Looking 10 to 15 years in the future, we foresee having very sophisticated and automated modeling, data preparation, and model management systems. During that time, we will also continue evolving the math and analytical techniques used. For such systems, we have typically approached horizontal problems first – marketing effectiveness, customer loyalty, manufacturing quality, cyber security, and so on. It will take another 20 to 30 years to perfect these systems.

Somewhere in that time window, we will start to build vertical applications for specific industries, such as automotive, healthcare, pharmaceutical, energy, security, and telecommunications. This will be a long, complex process.

Thus, in total, we foresee between 90 to 120 years' worth of work before we complete our analytics journey. Obviously, we have much to do, but thankfully the work has been both interesting and engaging.

CONCLUSION

Advanced analytics has come of age, as one company after another realizes the competitive necessity of the technology.

General Electric, for example, has recognized that advanced analytics will be the foundation for converting a giant of the Industrial Age into a formidable competitor in the Information Age. Indeed, the company's development of its Predix platform, with a mission of imbuing analytics in the offerings and operation of *every* GE business unit, is a significant bet and should cause all other businesses to take note.

In this chapter, we outlined many of the common analytical approaches and tools used by data scientists. To be sure, these technologies require specialist skills to master, but the approaches and techniques described are nothing but modern tools to achieve improved business performance.

Just as previous companies hired machinists and skilled trades people, you will hire data scientists, analysts, and very clever employees who will turn these analytical techniques into competitive advantage. You do not need to be an expert in advanced analytics, but you do need to invest and drive the process toward improved outcomes. In the following chapters, we'll describe just how to do that.

CHAPTER 3
The Age of the Algorithm
Economy

"The price of light is less than the cost of
darkness." – Arthur C. Nielsen, market researcher
and founder of ACNielsen

How much would any specific algorithm be worth to a company? Maybe $1,000? Or perhaps $10,000, or even $50,000? For Netflix, the answer was a cool $1 million.

More than 10 years ago, the online entertainment company was looking for a way to improve its video recommendation system for customers. It established the "Netflix Prize," an open competition with a $1 million purse. The cash would be awarded to anyone or group of individuals who could best improve the performance of Netflix's existing algorithm, called "Cinematch," by at least 10 percent.

The competition began on October 2, 2006, and three years later the winner was announced: BellKor's Pragmatic Chaos, a team that had developed an algorithm that was 10.06 percent better than Cinematch.[1]

Netflix's contest gained the company a better video recommendation system (as well as some nice free publicity for the firm), and it heightened people's awareness of the growing importance of algorithms in the business world.

But algorithms are not just responsible for recommending videos, restaurants, and books. Algorithms work silently behind the scenes of all manner of industries, sorting customer records, compressing data, encrypting information, and performing millions of other tasks essential to companies around the world.

In essence, we are currently living in the "algorithm economy," with people and businesses regularly consuming myriad algorithms every day.

But what exactly does that mean, and how did we get there? To understand how we've arrived at a time when an algorithm for recommending videos could be worth $1 million, we first need to take a step back and look at how the Internet has reshaped not just our global economy, but our society as a whole.

BEYOND THE DIGITAL ECONOMY

Author Don Tapscott coined the term "digital economy" in his 1995 bestseller "The Digital Economy,"[2] in which he described the Internet's impact on how companies operate and innovate. Since then, the definition of digital economy has grown wider to include all things digital, and Wikipedia now defines the term in the following way: "Digital economy refers to an economy that is based on digital computing technologies.... Increasingly, the 'digital economy' is intertwined with the traditional economy making a clear delineation harder."

Looking back to 1995, we can see clearly now that technology and data were embarking on a road of highly disruptive innovation unlike anything the world had seen before.

For one thing, everyone has become increasingly interconnected via the Internet and social media. In 1929, the Hungarian writer Frigyes Karinthy first wrote about the concept of "six degrees of separation," the idea that anyone on the planet can be connected to any other person through a chain of five other individuals. In 2011, researchers at Cornell, the Università degli Studi di Milano, and Facebook studied the "degrees" of connections among the 721 million people then using the social media website. They found that the average "degree" of connection was 3.74. Today that number has dropped to 3.57.[3]

Digital technology has certainly been connecting the dots between people, and it has also facilitated the growth of data that those relationships produce. As everyone becomes increasingly connected to devices such as smart phones, Fitbits, and connected cars, the volume of that data will only get larger – and more valuable.

According to one estimate, this new digital universe has been growing at 40 percent annually and is expected to continue doing so for the next decade. In fact, research by International Data Corp. predicts that the data created and copied annually will reach 44 zettabytes, or 44 trillion gigabytes, by 2020.[4] Our ability to create, capture and utilize this data is the cornerstone to the next disruptive economic shift.

IT'S NOT JUST ABOUT THE DATA

The phrase "data is the new oil" accurately captures just how important data has become; the increasing availability of big data has only helped to stoke people's excitement and enthusiasm. Back in 2001, industry analyst Doug Laney wrote the now-famous blog post that concentrated on the three "V"s of big data: volume, velocity, and variety.[5]

The ensuing debate over what exactly big data was (versus what it wasn't) was soon taking up virtually as much bandwidth as the technology that supported it. Joining that debate, many vendors tried to add their own proprietary "V"s to the equation, but this only confused the market and stalled the adoption of the technology.

For their part, many businesses have remained mystified by this "magical technology" that some claimed was a cure-all for anything data-related. The simple truth, however, is this: data by itself might be interesting and it may have many attributes, but the true value of such raw information will remain locked unless companies apply analytics to it to derive insights that will then lead to specific actions. Consequently, as the data proliferates and grows in volume, managing it will remain important, but leveraging it will become increasingly crucial – and doing so will take considerable business expertise to apply the appropriate analytics.

Perhaps Peter Sondergaard, senior vice president at technology research firm Gartner Inc. summarized it best in 2015: "Data is inherently dumb – Algorithms are where the real value lies. Algorithms define action."[6] Indeed, the ability to analyze and take actions is where the big payoff will come from data. It's the true part of the value proposition.

In other words, data might be the oil for fueling innovation, but companies need to refine value from it first; they do this by using analytics. And that's why Gartner is predicting that 75 percent of large and midsize organizations will be using advanced analytics and proprietary algorithms by 2020.[7] Simply put: the powerful combination of digital economy technologies coupled with the current avalanche of data is the foundation of the next economic shift – the algorithm economy.

Of course, companies have been using and managing algorithms for decades. But the traditional approaches were often historical, representing attempts to understand what happened in the past. Now that the technology exists and real-time data is available, firms can pivot from the historical to the contemporary, starting to better understand what is currently happening – and what may likely happen in the future.

CREATING PRODUCTS USING DATA AND INSIGHTS

The algorithm economy has gained solid traction on many fronts. Some applications are related to infrastructure and back-office functions, while others are customer facing. Netflix was willing to spend $1 million for an algorithm to improve its video recommendation service for its customers. Other companies have been investing in algorithms not just to improve their current product and service offerings, but also to extend them in innovative ways. These firms have been infusing their core product offerings with data collection and analytics to enhance their performance. Consider the following customer-facing examples of the algorithm economy in action:

- **Oral-B** has designed a Bluetooth-connected "Smart Toothbrush."[8] The product works with a consumer's smart phone to collect and analyze various data, enabling an algorithm to score that person's "performance" on oral hygiene and give real-time feedback. If, for example, a user is brushing too hard, he'll receive a recommendation to lighten up. The toothbrush will also track a person's brushing habits over time to determine if there's been any improvement, and that data can be shared with dental professionals.

- **BigBelly** has reinvented the public trash can.[9] The innovative new product is sensor driven and utilizes solar power for a built-in trash compactor that helps increase the container's capacity up to five times that of a traditional receptacle. In addition, wireless technology is used to send alerts when trash cans need emptying, and a Google-powered map application enables drivers to determine the most efficient service route. Overall the product saves time, fuel, and money, and the data collected can assist cities to better manage their trash removal efforts.

- **Starbucks** has used advanced analytics to extend its brand into a new market.[10] By analyzing customer data, point of sale (POS) information, and third-party market research, the company has created a new line of grocery-store products to reach customers inside their homes. For example, after learning that 25 percent of consumers don't add milk to their iced coffee at home, Starbucks began offering bottled unsweetened and sweetened iced coffee without milk or any other added flavors. Another finding was that more than 40 percent of customers don't add sugar to their tea, prompting the company to create two flavors of K-cups for unsweetened iced tea: mango green iced tea and peachy black tea. Starbucks is counting on these new products to help grow revenues by 10 percent annually through 2020.

We suspect that reinventing the toothbrush, garbage can, and coffee drinks might not seem like the most relevant success stories to executives who want their companies to benefit from the algorithm economy. But the key takeaway here is that *any* business can embed analytics and leverage data to create new products or enhance the value of their existing offerings. And as with any other worthy enterprise initiative, such projects can deliver a quantifiable return on investment (ROI) and add significant value to the bottom line.

REINVENTION THROUGH ALGORITHMS

Creating new products and services can certainly increase a company's competitiveness, but what is truly transformational are the various ways in which many firms are using the algorithm economy to reinvent themselves. Consider the following examples:

- **RioTinto** has created the mine of the future. Self-driving cars have recently been generating much media coverage, but RioTinto's Pilbara division has been using autonomous vehicles for years. The division deploys a fleet of nearly 70 autonomous haulage trucks along with automated drilling systems. An operations center in Perth enables all of the company's mines, ports, and rail systems to be operated from a single centralized location. In addition, the use of real-time data and an array of advanced analytics applications enable RioTinto to operate its mines with competitive efficiency that has improved its bottom line.

- **Telenor** has developed an entirely new line of business in the banking and finance field. Thanks to various technologies in the algorithm economy, the company now offers microloans for its mobile phone customers. To develop that line of business, a small team of data scientists leveraged customer usage data and risk models, applying them to consumers in emerging markets who didn't have credit cards or traditional bank relationships. In essence, Telenor was able to deploy advanced analytics to determine the credit worthiness of individuals who might not have qualified for traditional loans, resulting in the brand-new line of business in microloans.

- **General Electric** has designed a cloud platform specifically for industrial data and analytics.[11] The product, called Predix, is aimed at GE's customers in aviation, healthcare, energy, and transportation. Using the platform as a service (PaaS), firms can develop custom applications to utilize operational data from GE, resulting in better and faster decision making. Predix is an integral part of GE's overall strategy to build a significant software business that will enable the company to partner better with its customers. With Predix, GE has delivered a purpose-built solution that is quickly becoming a one-stop shop for analytics and insights that is essentially delivering the algorithm economy to GE clients.

Companies like RioTinto, Telenor, and GE are breaking new ground and leading the way in today's new algorithm economy. They are optimizing their operations and creating new solutions with data and analytics, setting them apart from the competition. These companies are enhancing their relationships with their core customers, bringing them new and critical services that are creating deeper and more valuable relationships.

DON'T REINVENT THE WHEEL – BORROW IT

What kind of in-house capabilities were necessary for companies like RioTinto and GE to succeed in their ambitious analytic initiatives? As with many new technologies, especially in the early adopter phase, the demand for skills in the algorithm economy has far outpaced the supply. However, that gap shouldn't deter businesses from implementing their own projects.

Most new economic models are built on a foundation that allows them to scale up. That foundation might be a specific technology, or it could be a cultural paradigm shift that supports the change. In the case of the algorithm economy, both of these play roles.

The technology that enables the algorithm economy to scale up is the very same thing that is at the core of the shift itself: the Internet and related digital technologies. The cultural shift is actually rooted in an economic model that has recently driven disruption around the world, giving birth to companies like Airbnb: namely, the "sharing economy," in which people borrow or rent an asset owned by someone else.

Application marketplaces are excellent examples of how the sharing economy is fueling the algorithm economy. Through these open marketplaces, data scientists and application developers share their analytic applications, models, and algorithms, and people can then leverage the sites to tap into the wisdom of crowds (that is, other data scientists). Data science professionals who want to speed their development cycles and achieve a faster time to value when building analytic solutions can utilize these communities to attain free or low-cost solutions that can be integrated into their projects.

These algorithm as a service (AaaS) platforms come in all shapes and sizes, with some focusing on specific industries or areas of expertise. Algorithmia, for example, is an open marketplace targeting application and algorithm developers. The site boasts more than 3,000 algorithms in its catalog and a powerful representational state transfer (REST) application programming interface (API) that allows developers to leverage their library and infuse their applications with ready-made analytics.[12] Algorithmia acts as a commerce enabler to its authors and users, empowering them to come together on a common platform. Transactions are billed on API calls; each time an application utilizes or calls an algorithm from the site, the user pays a credit to the author and to Algorithmia. The author sets the fee and Algorithmia executes the transaction. The library is extensive and covers text analysis, machine learning, data preprocessing, and computational mathematics.

Other marketplaces focus on specific languages or technologies. For instance, the Comprehensive R Archive Network (CRAN) website has thousands of projects, functions, and models for data scientists using the R language. The open source website is free to use, enabling many users to jumpstart their analytic projects. Through the site, R professionals have been sharing a variety of assets, including functions for actuarial scientists, Gaussian Mixture Models (GMMs), and constrained nonlinear optimizations.

And still other marketplaces are geared toward certain industries. Apervita, for example, contains algorithms and analytic applications for the healthcare industry. The website provides data scientists with a wide selection of clinical, operational, and financial analytics from leading health institutions. A powerful but easy-to-adopt REST API interface makes it easy for people to integrate algorithms and applications from the marketplace with other analytics solutions for wider deployment.

For the retail industry, Blue Yonder provides on-demand predictive analytics services. The cloud-based platform is designed to work with massive data volumes and delivers inventory replenishment and pricing optimization analytics. Retailers can use Blue Yonder to scale and extend their analytic environments to suit their needs, and tap into the industry expertise delivered by the company.

The sharing of industry expertise is also the foundation of Quantiacs, which enables those in the financial technology community to connect with one another. For years, innovation around automated trading platforms and the associated analytics has been ongoing, and now Quantiacs has opened up that knowledge to a wider group of users. The company's website provides "quant wannabes" with access to market data, enabling them to compete with others to refine their skills and train their platforms.

There are also marketplaces that focus on specific types of data. DataMapper, for example, is a unique marketplace for aerial drone video and photo analysis. The site has more than 50 partners that supply algorithms specific to mapping and agricultural analysis. A simple, downloadable user interface allows access to a deep library of algorithms, enabling people to purchase numerous applications for contour mapping, 2D map processing, and vegetation analysis.

The above examples are just a small sampling of how applications, models, data, and algorithms are becoming available across industries. Through such platforms, people can take advantage of reuse and speed to market without having to reinvent the wheel. Furthermore, the authors of those algorithms and applications can benefit from their expertise by renting or selling their intellectual property.

Companies have already begun to take advantage of these marketplaces, integrating them into their existing enterprise analytic solutions; this makes it easier for employees to leverage these sources of external intellectual property. This is especially important for firms that are looking to scale their analytic strategy and take advantage of the "wisdom of crowds" paradigm. That's why it's so critical for companies to ensure that their analytic solutions are open and extensible, so that they can take advantage of these resources.

Although the innovation cycle for these marketplaces is still in its early stage, we believe that in the future they will grow exponentially. This will open the door for faster ROIs for users and healthy revenue streams for authors.

The open source community has long been a pioneer in the area of open marketplaces. Websites like Algorithmia, CRAN, and Apervita will help provide the necessary infrastructure for the algorithm economy, much like the train tracks built by the railroad barons that led to new economic models in the mid-1800s. In essence, the infrastructure of algorithm marketplaces is the foundation needed for the mass adoption of advanced analytics as a major innovation disrupter in today's business environment.

ALGORITHMS GONE WILD

Of course, not every algorithm is designed to increase operational efficiency, enhance marketing programs, or improve customer service. In one of the more interesting applications, David Cope, a former professor of music, created "Emily Howell,"[13] a software program that "learns" how to compose original classical music. Apparently, the application has gotten so good at doing what it does that leading experts have been unable to differentiate Emily's music from compositions written by humans. Clips from Emily's latest album, "From Darkness, Light," are available on Amazon's website.[14]

Emily Howell's compositions are certainly impressive, but such sophisticated automation raises a number of issues. As much as the algorithm economy opens the door for compelling value propositions, companies will need to exercise caution and good governance as they rely increasingly on algorithmically-driven business models. All too often, people become enamored with a new technology, and fail to execute the proper due diligence when implementing it. Before deploying any algorithm, companies need to set the proper controls around it, ensuring that there are limits and stop gaps in place. Otherwise, the results could be disastrous.

Consider the cautionary tale of Knight Capital, a London-based financial services firm that specializes in executing trades for retail brokers. In August of 2012, Knight Capital's IT department executed a scheduled test of a new trading algorithm. The team took a conservative approach for the test, making sure to limit the application to only a handful of stocks. Moreover, to prevent the possibility of the application actually executing trades, the buy/sell points were set well outside where the markets were then trading.

But then, during the test of the application, something went terribly wrong. The complex, algorithmically driven platform started to execute live trades. One of the stocks that was in the trading profile was energy utility Exelon, and the stock had a bid/ask spread of 0.15 cents per share. Unfortunately for Knight Capital, the trading platform was buying Exelon and selling it immediately at a 0.15 cents per share loss. That might not sound like much, but the software was trading blocks of Exelon at 40 trades per second, 2,400 times each minute. The result: in just 45 minutes, Knight Capital had lost $440 million,[15] which almost put the company out of business.

Even technologically savvy leaders can make mistakes. In August of 2016, Facebook decided to use an algorithm to replace the human editorial team for its Facebook Trending News area.[1] The human editors had been responsible for curating the stream of trending news, writing descriptions and helping to ensure the quality of the stream of information.

The change to using an algorithm was well-intentioned, as Facebook had been receiving negative feedback that its editorial team lacked neutrality. Not long after the launch, though, several totally false "news" stories slipped past the logic of the algorithm, winding up at the top of Facebook's trending news. One was a completely fake story about Fox News host Megyn Kelly, another focused on the political commentator Ann Coulter, and a third was about a sexually graphic video that involved a McDonald's McChicken sandwich. The glitch has since been fixed, but it nevertheless caused Facebook an embarrassing black eye in the court of public opinion for failing to apply the right governance to its editorial algorithm.[16]

Algorithmic automation was the culprit in another blunder involving the online giant Amazon. Third-party merchants that supply products to Amazon's website often control their list prices with automated algorithms. A book vendor named Bordeebook benefited from a large amount of positive customer feedback, so it was able to charge a bit more for its products, apparently setting its pricing algorithm to 1.270589 times that of its closest competitor, Profnath.[17] For its part, Profnath was using a similar algorithm, but had evidently set it to maintain a 0.9983 price as compared to Bordeebook.

Things got out of hand when both merchants tried to sell the out-of-print book "The Making of a Fly: The Genetics of Animal Design," which was normally priced around $70.00. As each vendor's algorithm worked its magic, the price of that academic book started to skyrocket, hopscotching all the way past $23 million. Not surprisingly, no one bought the book for that exorbitant sum, and eventually the two vendors realized the error and brought their stratospheric "The Making of a Fly" prices back down to Earth.

CONCLUSION

As Knight Capital, Facebook, and many others have discovered, competing in the algorithm economy is not for the faint of heart. The lesson here is that as firms become more sophisticated in their utilization of algorithms, they must also become increasingly adept in the controlling and governance of those applications. In the coming years, many companies will likely make mistakes in doing so, but the smarter ones will handle those tasks with skill, infusing their organizations with advanced analytics to provide greater insights and the ability to act at the speed of business.

The simple truth is that people are consuming algorithms every day, increasingly cultivating an acceptance of and appetite for them. In fact, most consumers don't want to understand the inner workings of a software application, but they want to benefit from the insights and actions that algorithms can generate.

Abstracting that complexity is a key reason why analytics is so important today. Countless applications must run and execute quietly in the background, becoming part and parcel of many everyday processes. People have come to expect, for example, that their e-commerce shopping experience will keep track of their past purchases, notify them on the progress of new purchases, and recommend future or additional purchases based on their behavior.

These types of interactions are at the heart of why businesses are advancing more toward delivering analytically driven experiences, and this movement represents a cultural shift that is one of the key drivers of the algorithm economy. In the following chapters, we will explore exactly how numerous companies have been adapting to – if not actively thriving in – this new environment.

Endnotes:

[1] http://bit.ly/2isrCft.

[2] Don Tapscott, "The Digital Economy: Promise and Peril in the Age of Networked Intelligence" (New York: McGraw-Hill, 1997).

[3] http://bit.ly/1Sveg1b February, 2016.

[4] http://bit.ly/2jMfjOq April 2014.

[5] http://gtnr.it/QI1CxJ.

[6] http://gtnr.it/1ONf6EA, The Algorithm Economy Webcast.

[7] Data shared at 2016 BI and Analytics Summit in Munich.

[8] http://bit.ly/1fD5ntK.

[9] http://bit.ly/2towLOE.

[10] https://yhoo.it/2btPxav.

[11] http://bit.ly/2tXDc8c.

[12] http://bit.ly/2s1jfMB.

[13] http://bit.ly/2tkqt1N.

[14] http://amzn.to/2t0slug.

[15] http://bit.ly/2s1vrgb.

[16] http://bit.ly/2t0vIkN.

[17] http://bit.ly/2uiaGh2.

CHAPTER 4
The Modern Data
Ecosystem

"Sometimes it's the journey that teaches you a lot
about your destination."– Drake

Of course, every company would like to minimize the number
and size of its customer delinquent and default payments. One
firm that has actually been accomplishing that is Danske Bank,
a leading financial institution in northern Europe with five
million customers.

Thanks to advanced analytics and the use of a variety of data –
not just information from customers, but also from external
sources like credit bureaus – Danske Bank is able to better
predict whether a particular loan applicant will default within a
year.[1] Moreover, the company is able to respond quickly to any
loan application, 24 by 7 by 365; the bank doesn't simply

respond with a denial or approval, but with specific credit limits that are both fair and accurate.

To accomplish this, Danske Bank has deployed a leading-edge commercial analytic platform, along with a refined process for building and deploying credit-risk models in half the time of older models.[1] Those analytic models are updated regularly with the availability of new data, and the results have been impressive. The firm has been able to gain market share and improve customer satisfaction, all without suffering any increase in the customer default or delinquency rates.

Danske Bank is hardly alone. In industry after industry, companies are deploying advanced analytics to gain competitive advantage. Indeed, as we discussed in Chapter 1, a shift has been occurring that is nearly impossible to ignore – from both an IT and business standpoints. Call it a "perfect storm" of disruption in our data ecosystems that is forcing companies of all sizes to sit up and take notice.

On the surface, each of the four main drivers of that storm – maturing users, new technologies, decreasing cost barriers, and abundant data – may not seem to be significantly disruptive. Together, however, they have been dramatically reshaping the analytic playing field.

In the modern data ecosystem of today, companies like Danske Bank deploy data and advanced analytics not only to increase the efficiency and quality of their existing operations, but also to offer innovative and compelling products and services. To appreciate the foundation of such capabilities, let's take a closer look at each of those four main drivers.

Figure 4.1 The four drivers of the modern data ecosystem.

1. MATURING USERS

The first driver is a maturing user community. In and of itself, this trend doesn't seem too surprising; as technologies evolve, so do users. Moreover, as data becomes more accessible, the user community evolves to consume and apply that data. In the specific case of data analytics users, though, this maturation appears to be happening at blinding speed.

All across the typical enterprise, people want to get their hands-on data and the insights that can be derived from it. And while the population of users is growing, so is their level of sophistication. A few years back, business users settled for the "queue up and wait" style of analytics. They would review a report, gain a bit of insight based on the historical data, and take their question to a data expert who had the specialized tools, data access, and skill set to help them get to the next level of insight. Then it could (and often did) take days or weeks for the answer to come back, and that delay eroded or altogether eliminated the value of that information. The question might have changed over the intervening time, or the answer might have been rendered irrelevant by evolving business conditions. Users today are of an entirely different breed. They are no longer content to be sitting on the sidelines, waiting for their analytic insights to be delivered to them.

Now line of business (LOB) executives have joined the action, consuming analytics in new ways. They have grown to understand the power of business intelligence (BI) since the last economic downturn. They have discovered that although BI isn't recession-proof, it enables companies to find new and clever ways to be competitive, serve customers better, and react more nimbly to changing markets. Today, these same professionals are looking to apply analytics in the same way to drive their companies forward. Indeed, since the dawn of the big data revolution, there's been a noticeable shift toward LOBs leading the spending, initiating more projects than IT. From one company to the next, the finance, marketing, sales, and customer service LOBs are now spearheading the investments in data and analytics.

At the same time, the BI, business, and IT analyst roles have also evolved. These professionals now consume and deliver the outcomes of analytics, acting much like bridges between the business and the IT sides of the organization. They facilitate smooth transitions of data, and help others understand the information so that real insights are delivered and actions can be planned and executed.

In addition, the developer community is also playing a new role in consuming analytics and embedding those insights into widespread applications. In fact, many end users of these applications are unaware that they are even utilizing the output of highly sophisticated advanced algorithms within their day-to-day work processes.

Finally, the data scientists and "citizen data scientists" are relatively new to the data ecosystem, but bring a new set of demands and needs. They are often referred to as "data unicorns" because they are seemingly mythical with respect to their unique combination of expertise and skill sets. We'll talk about them in greater detail in Chapter 5.

As with any revolution, the new guard has found itself quickly at odds with the establishment. An analyst friend of ours once depicted this struggle as the war of the hoodies and the suits. The "hoodies" represent the new breed of analytic and data consumer. These new users arrive in the enterprise with a different set of expectations that run counter to the established practices and rules set forth by the tenured and experienced IT and business professionals – the "suits."

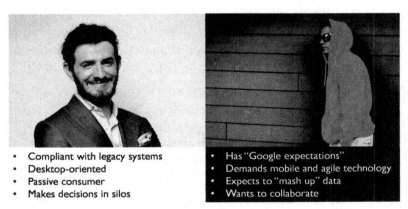

- Compliant with legacy systems
- Desktop-oriented
- Passive consumer
- Makes decisions in silos

- Has "Google expectations"
- Demands mobile and agile technology
- Expects to "mash up" data
- Wants to collaborate

Figure 4.2 The "suits" versus the "hoodies".

Generally speaking, the hoodie users have greater expectations. They expect free access to data and want very much to collaborate with peers, often "mashing up" data in ways that the establishment sees as risky and difficult to manage. For their part, the "suits" have good reason to protect their systems; they are typically driven by system performance concerns and regulatory issues that the "hoodie" crowd might see as overly restrictive and limiting.

The disruption caused by this inherent conflict between the two sets of users will require deft managerial skills to resolve. On one hand, the hoodie users will come to the table with a list of demands including access to new data sources, use cases to consume real-time data, flexible environments that support new use cases, collaborative and iterative environments that move as fast as they do, and freedom in implementing new projects. On the other hand, the suits will attempt to control the environment and implement systems to manage it, and their demands will typically emphasize greater security and control, governance and compliance, auditable data use, testing and stability, proven enterprise processes, and data quality.

It's important to note here that as the user community evolves it also grows, and this growth will make for some interesting changes as well. In the early days of analytics, the community was well-defined. Today, the job titles of those involved in analytics are varied. With this variety comes a diversity of needs that test the bounds of traditional platforms and systems.

Ultimately, this is a discussion about the democratization of access, tools, and data. The trend is toward increasing numbers of people within the organization being interested in data-driven insights, and these new workloads are creating changes in our data architectures and the systems that support data and analytics across the enterprise. This shift is happening to companies of all sizes. Ignoring these new demands will put a firm's data environment at risk, leaving its business vulnerable to competitors who are willing to take on the challenge and democratize how they deliver and support analytics.

2. NEW TECHNOLOGIES

New technologies typically enable change, but they can also act as disruptive forces for challenging and improving traditional processes. This is especially true in the world of analytics, where recent technological advances have allowed companies to do more in smarter and faster ways.

Moreover, they have helped businesses to innovate with data and information in ways that were previously restricted by technology (or at the very least, not very well supported by it). As described in Chapter 1, technologies such as data warehouses and business intelligence allow firms to store and access data in relational structures, and to use software platforms to look at historical information. Today, companies can harness new technologies that enable them to address *all* of the data within their ecosystem, and to work at much greater scale and speed than previously possible.

As the proverbial saying goes, necessity is the mother of invention; that was certainly true when it came to advanced analytics. Here, Google and Yahoo played pivotal roles in bringing about a new framework to handle what was once thought of as unmanageable. The two Internet companies were at the epicenter of the big data revolution in 2003. At the time, they needed new scalable solutions to handle petabytes of data; this need brought about the invention of open source technologies like Hadoop. Data warehouses gave way to platforms with new flexibilities and features for dealing with analytics and much larger and more diverse datasets.

The new mantra among progressive data analytic professionals is to position data on the best possible platform for the best possible use. This course of action runs in the face of traditional strategies, which often forced people to fit or transform data into enterprise data warehouse structures that had difficulties meeting the use cases applied by analytics. Moreover, such conventional approaches are not well-suited to handling today's much larger and more diverse data sources. By adopting the new mantra of best platform for best use, data professionals can allow the "gravity" of data to dictate the proper platform. Having a technology like Hadoop that is custom-designed to today's big data challenges allows companies to incorporate greater levels of data into their analytics, providing deeper insights and better courses of action. Furthermore, Hadoop is only one of many newer technologies that have arrived this past decade to enable novel approaches to analytics. In our experience, we have found that companies are fulfilling and serving their use cases for advanced analytics by using a hybrid mix of traditional and new solutions.

The bottom line is that new platforms, coupled with in-memory analytical capabilities, enable companies to analyze data at a greater scale and a faster speed. NoSQL solutions, for example, have sufficient speed to integrate insights and actions into systems that move in real time. In the end, technology has caught up with demand, adapting to fit new use cases and myriad opportunities, enabling analytics at the speed and scale of today's businesses.

3. DECREASING COST BARRIERS

Financial barriers have long kept many companies on the sidelines of unleashing the true power of data analytics. Small firms have been forced to wait for some level of commoditization so they could get into the game. This is certainly happening in the areas of big data and analytics.

As mentioned earlier, new technologies like Hadoop and NoSQL have come from the open source community, and they have come with a "free" price tag.

Part of the marketing buzz surrounding these technologies has been their affordability. In the past, a company had to obtain a government grant to execute a big data and analytic project, and that's exactly where many of those initiatives started. Early research on the human genome, for example, was fueled by grants and government funding to help push innovation forward. Today, companies of all sizes can afford to embark on new, analytically-driven projects that in the past had been cost prohibitive.

We would be remiss, however, if we didn't issue a caveat. Although these new technologies are knocking down cost barriers as well as project risks, to say that they are free is inaccurate.

When you were a kid, perhaps you saw a sign on our neighbor's lawn that read "Free Puppies," and you raced home to use the "free" argument with your parents. At first glance, this appears to be the case with many of these new technologies. But your parents were right: Hadoop and NoSQL may offer a low barrier to adoption, but require considerable care and feeding, just like any puppy.

Unfortunately, there's a noticeable skills gap in the industry around these technologies; as utilization grows, that gap will have a financial impact on many businesses. As such, executives should be wary of implementing any new technology-driven project without understanding the *total* cost of ownership.

With that one important caveat noted, overall these new technologies are allowing a wider and more diverse group of companies to compete in the analytics and big data space, causing a new wave of disruption coupled with an economic advantage.

4. ABUNDANT DATA

In the 1990s, data professionals focused on centralizing data. This involved moving it from source systems through complicated extract, transform, and load (ETL) scenarios and data quality processes, and eventually delivering that information to enterprise data warehouses. These data warehouse infrastructures were rigidly maintained and designed to be a single source of truth for data and simple analytic consumption. The frameworks that governed data warehouses lacked agility and often proved costly to maintain. Simple changes to datasets often required the approval of committees and rarely kept up with the requests of the data consumer.

And it's not just that those data warehouses were strictly controlled; they also lacked the capability to handle diverse sources of information. Indeed, the 80/20 rule has been applied to enterprise data for longer than people care to remember. Countless articles have been published about the hurdles to tapping into that 80 percent of data that is highly unstructured and difficult to leverage in traditional systems. (This includes e-mail, customer call records, contracts, and social data, to name just a few of those sources.) The hard truth was that the expense, lack of technology, and impracticality of using such additional data sources forced companies to ignore valuable information that could have been gleaned from their environments.

Now, with recent technology advances, companies can leverage data from a much wider and more distributed landscape, allowing for greater and deeper insights. Introducing more data into an analytic environment brings about new challenges, sure, but overall the addition can substantially augment ongoing projects and open the floodgates for companies to pursue new and exciting directions. Today, the more advanced companies are taking a hybrid approach, including both unstructured data and structured data in their analytic initiatives.

ECOSYSTEM CHALLENGES

The forces of this perfect storm − maturing users, new technologies, decreasing cost barriers, and abundant data − are causing companies to reassess their approaches to analytics. The smarter firms have been finding new ways to drive revenue and serve customers. Now that we understand the why and how of this new approach to data and analytics, we need to take a step back and consider the various challenges therein.

As the data that companies use becomes increasingly diverse and more widely distributed, executives must manage and control that new environment with respect to security, service level agreements (SLAs), global and regional laws concerning data and analytics, and compliance and regulatory issues. In addition, firms will also face challenges managing a distributed and increasingly complex analytic environment. Early on, most companies were leveraging only a handful of algorithms to drive their business. Now, it's common for them to have hundreds or even thousands of models in play at any given time. This makes model management and optimization critical to growing an organization's analytic environment.

In any analytics project, companies must determine what data to use and where that information should reside. Perhaps even more importantly, they also need to decide where to locate the analytics. Once a firm is operating within a hybrid data environment, the same concepts should be applied to its analytics. In other words, putting the right data on the right platform is important, but an advantage can also be gained by putting the right analytics in the right place.

Defaulting back to the traditional approach of placing all analytics at the center of a company's data ecosystem is not only restrictive; it can also limit the firm's analytic capabilities. Instead, placing the analytics in a database or in the same place the data is originating from can provide a path to controlling and filtering the data and, perhaps more importantly, the opportunity to apply analytics in real or "right" time. That capability can confer significant competitive advantage, as we will describe in Chapter 9.

Figure 4.3 shows a map of the modern data ecosystem. In the figure, the users on the outside represent the new community of individuals who are driving the different types of analytics shown in the first ring. Here, data lives where gravity takes it, or where it best aligns to today's new platforms. The managerial challenges are highlighted in the next ring: data integration and information management. The inner bubbles are the different factors that must be considered. How will you load data? Is it structured or unstructured? What type of speed of response is required from the analytics? How complex is the overall workload and are you restricted by cost? Each of those considerations will drive the hybrid data ecosystem and help users to decide where work will get done.

In general, we recommend a flexible approach with a centralized analytics platform that brings with it the ability to transport the analytics to the data or database for execution. Consider, for example, the Internet of Things (IoT). The sensors that drive IoT are almost always found well outside of traditional data environments – in cars, on oil rigs, in the

operating room, or on the manufacturing floor of a factory —
and the volume of information flowing from them can be
overwhelming.

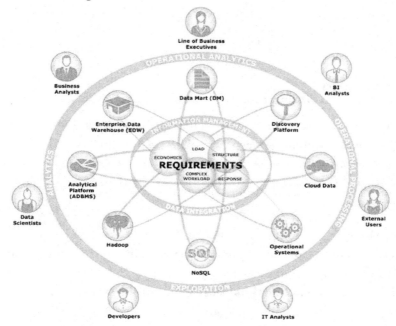

Figure 4.3 The modern data ecosystem.[2]

For instance, some manufacturing processes have upwards of
10,000 sensors monitoring a wide array of functions. If each of
those devices takes a reading once a second, then that would
amount to 864 million rows of data every day. Even if the
individual data reading from each sensor were only a couple of
kilobytes, the volume would still be tremendous, and the task of
moving that information across a network would become
cumbersome and expensive.

Instead of transporting that raw data, a better alternative
might be to apply analytics at its origin. Utilizing such "edge
analytics" is a powerful approach to managing the new data
ecosystem. The capability to "listen" to data and respond in

real time makes it possible for companies to adapt quickly to changing conditions in the market, on the plant floor, in customer environments, and elsewhere. Such systems are becoming critical for businesses to stay nimble and responsive in today's diverse and disparate data landscapes.

CONCLUSION

The business environment is changing faster than ever before. How can companies keep up? The answer lies in advanced analytics, which empower firms to not only respond quickly to market changes but also to anticipate them with greater accuracy.

In the past, building the capacity for such advanced analytics was feasible for only large corporations with significant resources and abundant capital. Today, thanks to the four drivers of the modern data ecosystem, medium- and small-sized firms can also play the analytics game. As we shall see in Chapter 8, those businesses that are successful in their efforts will have the flexibility to protect margins, hold market share, and compete in innovative ways to truly differentiate their offerings from the competition.

Endnotes:

[1] "Bank Speeds Time to Market with Advanced Analytics," available at http://dell.to/2t0q0PP.

[2] "Modern Data Ecosystem," Shawn Rogers & John Myers, Enterprise Management Associates - http://bit.ly/2toBjVi.

CHAPTER 5
Analytics Takes a Village: Building and Enabling the Right Team

"Be short in speech and restrained in action." – Marcus Aurelius

Cisco is a well-known leader in the field of networking, technology, and enterprise solutions. The company is also a cutting-edge organization in the use of advanced analytics, having recently established its Center for Predictive Analytics and Decision Science. The center is run by Robert Lake, a senior data scientist who's a vocal proponent of building a learning culture that's diverse and technically skilled but focused on solving business problems. Lake's team of a dozen people comprises a mix of men and women, experienced staff members and recent graduates, who are adept at using a variety of languages and tools, including R, Python, Statistica, and other commercial as well as open source software.

Such technological expertise notwithstanding, the team's focus is on addressing *business* issues and not technical ones. Business problems are proposed by the various operating units of Cisco, and the team members self-organize to thoroughly understand the business objectives and to find solutions. The Center provides skills, resources, and guidance on a project basis and, once a solution has been developed and implemented, the requesting business unit will own that work. Specifically, after a solution has been built and deployed, the team at the Center will teach staffers in the business unit how to run and maintain that application on a daily basis.

Thus far, Cisco's analytics center has provided a number of solutions for the company's various functions. These functions range from manufacturing to marketing to distribution, and the turnaround times have been extremely impressive. In the past, analytics projects would take an average of perhaps nine months from start to finish. Today, Lake pushes his team to provide solutions within a single day.

Of course, the team needs to scope the challenge and understand the decisions to be made, but once that prep work is completed, the goal for the majority of cases is to complete the modeling work in one day. That kind of lightning-fast turnaround has enabled Cisco to better understand its business and make quick adjustments when necessary.

When the company investigated its customer churn, for example, the analytics team uncovered distinct patterns for specific customer segments and product types. As it turned out, certain customers who were using a particular type of service were defecting after two years when, instead, Cisco could have been migrating those customers to a new product type. Now

Cisco can take advantage of these previously missed opportunities, thanks to the powerful insights generated by the analytics team.

ANALYTIC CENTERS OF EXCELLENCE (COEs)

In our experience, the companies that have had the greatest success in deploying data analytics have implemented a hybrid model to build their analytics teams. The foundation of that model is typically some variation of the following: a strong, central center of excellence (like Cisco's Center for Predictive Analytics and Decision Science) that is managed by a seasoned and experienced analytics professional and expert (like Robert Lake).

The center of excellence (COE) represents a tipping point from the old to new paradigms that have supported analytically-driven companies. This shift mirrors a similar disruption that occurred in the business intelligence (BI) space when users who were no longer intimidated by the technology pushed for greater control and ownership of the data and resulting insights. This upheaval left some BI vendors in the dust (for example, Cognos and Business Objects) and opened the door for entrants with new disruptive products (for example, Qlik and Tableau).

The analytic COE should bring together the expert skillsets required to democratize the use of analytics across the organization. The goal is to spread the best practices, tools, and processes that will make analytics easier for people to deploy and leverage.

When implemented effectively, the COE provides a middle ground between two extreme paradigms. In the old way, the business units had to place orders for new analytics models and then wait for weeks or even months. In the new way, the situation was akin to the "wild, wild West," with people haphazardly using analytics tools without fully understanding them, resulting in misleading insights. Effective COEs reign in those two extremes by eliminating bottlenecks while also maintaining quality control over the tools used and the results generated.

To accomplish that, the COE must build standardized templates, widgets, workflows, reusable models, and visualizations that people can easily customize for their specific purposes. These reusable assets, which must be organized and made available throughout the organization, could be like analytics "ger-animals," essentially color-coded and easy for people to assemble together. The ease-of-use characteristic of the modules will not only empower data scientists but also help create a population of "citizen data scientists," thus bridging the gap between IT and the various business units.

Another key requirement here is data access and preparation, with the COE becoming the supplier or curator for data and insights. All these responsibilities of the COE are critical parts of a company's strategy to scale analytics across the business.

THE CHIEF ANALYTICS OFFICER

The COE is headed by the chief analytics officer (CAO), sometimes called the chief data officer (CDO). Ideally, this individual is a vice president or senior-level position reporting directly to the CEO, with responsibility for analytics across the global enterprise (see figures below illustrating three possible organizational models).

The CAO is the point person to ensure that all analytics initiatives are aligned and that the organization is investing and driving toward the same (or substantially similar) goals in all analytics projects and work. But the CAO is not a gatekeeper; he or she is more of a guide, coordinator, and supporter. This person helps the line-of-business executives understand how to achieve synergy by leveraging data analytics and by creating an analytics culture of constant improvement across the organization.

The CAO should be an individual with years of experience as an analytics practitioner, resulting in a strong sense of the following: what can realistically be accomplished with data and analytics, the timing of developing analytics, and the reality of putting analytics into production systems. The CAO should be on a peer level with the business unit leaders, enabling him or her to speak directly with those senior executives about investments in analytics and the returns that can be expected.

As head of the COE, the CAO must help to frame all challenges and projects in a way that maximizes their benefits to the organization. As an example, the marketing group might ask for a customer segmentation analysis by buying patterns and revenue, and the customer success group might request a customer segmentation analysis by return levels and revenue.

The CAO is in the position to see that these two requests are very closely related and should be executed as one initiative with two sets of outputs. Thus, by having the CAO and the COE team oversee all analytics work, the organization will be better able to achieve synergies, reduce costs, and increase the throughput of such projects.

COE ORGANIZATIONAL MODELS

As a relatively new position, it would be rare to have the CAO reporting to the CEO, but that is not set in stone. If the organization feels strongly about analytics and the value to be derived, the CAO could report directly to the CEO.

Typically, the CAO/CDO would report to the CTO. Aligning the CAO and CTO is best due to the rapidly evolving nature of analytics and the innovative aspect of analytics. The CTO and CAO will work together to ensure that the current and future state of the companies' - technology, processes and infrastructure can and will work seamlessly as analytics are added at multiple levels and across numerous processes in the operations of the organization.

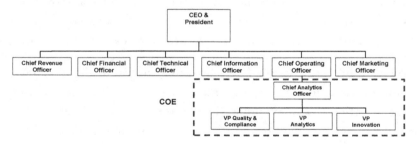

Figure 5.1 Possible organization for COE.

If the organization does not have a CTO, having the CAO report to the COO is best due wide-ranging impact analytics will have on the companies' - technology, processes and infrastructure.

The COO & CAO can work together to anticipate and plan for the impact that analytics will have as they are added at multiple levels and across numerous processes in the operations of the organization.

Also, the financial requirements and resources needed will require a reallocation of costs and budgets, the COO has the authority and ability to make the needed changes to enable the mission of the CAO and COE to be realized.

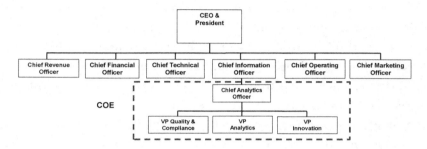

Figure 5.2 Least desirable, but possible organization for COE.

Having the CAO report to the CIO is possible, but it limits the scope, scale and impact of the role significantly.

The CIO & CAO can work together, but in all likelihood, the impact of analytics will be lessened as the analytics mission is rendered inferior to the IT agenda of running systems and ensuring SLAs are met.

The role of the CIO and IT has evolved into a role of managing systems and not driving or delivering innovation and change, but the nature of the role and mission, the CIO and IT are not a natural fit for the CAO, COE or the analytics mission.

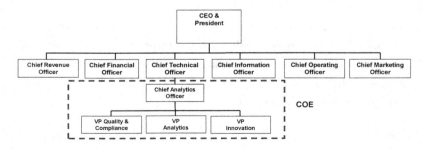

Figure 5.3 Optimal organization for COE.

THE COE STAFF

The COE should be staffed primarily with analysts, or data scientists, who possess a wide range of skills and aptitudes. These individuals must focus on the process of converting data into information, and information into insights, on a regular and repeatable basis. Their skillsets should be diverse, combining knowledge in computer science, applied math, statistics, and expertise in different subject matters like marketing and finance. It's rare to find all of those attributes in a single person, and that's why such individuals have been dubbed the "unicorns" of the data world.

The term "data scientist" itself is the new and updated label for roles that had been previously referred to as "analysts." The moniker is not a simple relabeling of an existing role – although, of course, there is a bit of repackaging. (The running joke is that if you want to add up to $100,000 to your annual salary, change your title to "data scientist.") That said, data scientists do differ from their analyst predecessors in several important ways.

In the past, analysts were isolated, and responsible for just a portion of the analytic process. They might have been in the IT group or in a line-of-business function like marketing. Their primary responsibility was to build a model (or an ensemble of models) to achieve a stated business goal.

That goal might have been, for example, to reduce customer churn by 20 percent in 90 days. So, the analysts would gather and integrate the necessary data, build and test the model, validate the results in the test environment, and alert management that the model was complete.

There's no question that these tasks require a substantial amount of effort and coordination across numerous business functions. However, it's also very clear that none of the processes as described above includes any real-world factors or context that would have a measurable impact on the stated business goal. All the analysts' work would result in a model, but not necessarily in any change in business processes or in any impact on customer churn. Historically, this has been the crux of one of the main gripes of the profession: lots of work, with little to no actual change in operations.

In contrast, data scientists are responsible for everything that analysts used to do *and* they must also implement the models in production systems. That is, data scientists own the entire process, from the formulation of a business objective and goals to the accomplishment of those goals. They are held responsible for achieving business results (such as reducing customer churn by 20 percent in 90 days), not just simply implementing checklists of technical items. The perspective of data scientists has accordingly shifted away from a narrow focus on technology to a wider emphasis on improving the business.

To summarize, analysts were tasked with developing models that had the potential to change business outcomes, but rarely were they held accountable for ensuring that the models actually improved operations toward those goals. Data scientists, by contrast, are accountable for the *entire* lifecycle of an analytic project, including the achievement of the stated business goals.

So, why are analysts limited in their roles while data scientists are not? Several factors help explain the difference. The first is historical timing. In the past, computer systems, technology stacks, security environments, and other variables were all developed and implemented to maintain control over data, processes, and people. These were not designed with the idea of a data scientist cutting across all areas to access and leverage data from a wide range of sources.

The second factor is technology. Security systems, data preparation environments, analytical tools, and visualization systems have all evolved. Today, security systems can provide flexible access to individuals or small groups of people, allowing them granular-level permission on a permanent or temporary basis. This enables employees to access data in a way that's appropriate only for their analytical purposes.

At the same time, data preparation, analytical tools, and visualization software have made huge strides in the ability for non-technical users to build, revise, extend, and maintain analytical workflows. As recently as just five years ago, a highly skilled and trained team was needed to build any sort of analytical workflow. Today, a summer intern can build reasonably complicated workflows with minimal supervision.

The third factor is talent. In 2010, one of us (Thompson) was asked to review the proposed curriculum of a new undergraduate program in data analytics. It was one of only a few such programs being considered. Today, it would be difficult to find a major university (and possibly even a second-tier college) that does not have a complete program or courses geared toward teaching data analysis skills. Even high schools are now offering courses in analytics and data analysis. The time has passed when analysts had Ph.D. degrees and were part of a specialized group. Data scientists are now part of every operating unit at some companies, and the talent needed for these roles is being developed starting at the high school level.

Yet, given all this recent push in education, is there a talent shortage? Unfortunately, the answer is yes, and it is indeed a problem – although not an insurmountable one. The dialog most often heard is that a foreign country – China, India, or some other country – will surpass the United States economically because U.S. students aren't being sufficiently trained in science and math.

That argument oversimplifies the basic issues. Yes, the United States does need to increase the numbers of its college graduates with science, technology, engineering, and math (STEM) degrees. But it's also important to understand that many technical tasks can be automated, and even more will be in the coming years. After all, when the first man landed on the moon, slide rules played an important role. Today, they are nothing more than interesting antiques.

The point is that advances in software, hardware, processes, and other technologies will make analytics more accessible to a wider range of people, not just those with specialized, arcane knowledge. Indeed, companies no longer have to search for "unicorn" data scientists because of the increasing democratization of the analytics field, which has led to the emergence of a growing population of "citizen data scientists." We will discuss that trend in detail later in this chapter.

DIFFERENT DATA SCIENTIST ROLES

Ideally, an analytics COE should contain a mix of data scientists and other staffers with different backgrounds and areas of expertise. A good starting team would include people in the following roles:

- **Data management experts.** These individuals have experience in being the employees or team members that most often interface to the IT function or staff. They know how to explain and describe the data requirements for the wide range of analytics that will be executed over time.

They should be well-versed in accessing, integrating, and working with data from internal as well as external sources. They should know how to obtain the data themselves, but be prepared and ready to work through the IT function if needed. It is common for the majority of the effort required in an analytical project to be spent in the phase referred to as data preparation, data management, data integration, or even data "wrangling."

- **An R expert.** R is a programming language that's oriented toward analytics and analytical applications. It has become the *lingua franca* of analytics – younger professionals who want to work in the data science field, as well as the great majority of students who will be graduating from university, are (or will soon be) fluent in R.

- **A Python expert.** Another very popular language is Python. Although it's not specifically deployed in analytics, Python is a scripting language that's often used in conjunction with R. Python is very powerful and useful for building data management routines and for other tasks that are required to build complete analytical workflows.

- **Experts in major vendors' tools.** Proprietary systems from SAS, IBM, Statistica, and other vendors are not going to disappear, and it may very well be the case that your organization supports more than one. These systems confer benefits around security, governance, and standardization. Beyond those, it's often the case that when new staff members come to work for your organization, they will want to continue using the tools that they are familiar with. To keep those employees as productive as possible, companies should consider supporting as many of these tools as necessary.

- **A visualization expert.** Great analytics are worthless if they
  cannot be understood and used. Visualization and
  presentation software has taken off in the past few years.
  There are many options for displaying compelling
  interactive graphical depictions of analytical output.
  Narrative generation is another useful tool for explaining
  analytical results. It's important to remember that people
  will have their individual preferences for tabular
  (spreadsheet), graphical (dashboards), or narrative (text)
  style output. The visualization expert on your team should
  understand the wide range of technologies available and the
  optimal methods that your teams need to use to obtain,
  consume and understand the output of the various
  analytical systems being used in your organization.

In addition to the above roles, the COE would also benefit from
staff members with expertise in Bayesian approaches, neural
networks, deep learning, and ensemble modeling. Such an array
of individuals will provide a solid foundation of analytic
capabilities, which companies can greatly supplement with the
addition of another type of talent: citizen data scientists.

CITIZEN DATA SCIENTISTS

Recently, the technology research firm Gartner Inc. coined the
term "citizen data scientist" to describe "a person who creates
or generates models that leverage predictive or prescriptive
analytics but whose primary job function is outside of the field
of statistics and analytics." A citizen data scientist's primary
job function could, for example, be a line-of-business role or an
IT position, but one who uses statistics and analytics to
supplement their daily work. Without a doubt, citizen data
scientists have been playing a crucial role in the new analytics
ecosystem inside many companies.

In the ecosystem, the chief analytics officer (CAO) runs the center of excellence (COE), which serves the analytical needs of the entire organization on a global basis and acts as the nerve center for all analytics design. The COE might employ citizen data scientists to work alongside the experienced data scientists, and the different line-of-business (LoB) units may also include their own citizen data scientists.

The regular data scientists are experts in applying analytical techniques and algorithms to solve difficult data- and math-oriented problems. They'll typically have years of experience in building analytical solutions to deliver business results.

Citizen data scientists may not have the same technological expertise or experience, but they are experts in business problems. They understand analytical techniques, and they are skilled in using analytical technologies to solve problems. Moreover, they are adept at working with the LoB staff, the IT professionals, the COE staff, and others to ensure that projects come together in a manner that solves the stated business goals.

The citizen data scientists own the business problem and the process to solve it. They are responsible for building the necessary analytics or models, either from building blocks provided by the COE or from scratch, using their own skills and abilities. As mentioned earlier, many citizen data scientists will work in a LoB function – such as marketing, sales, logistics, or manufacturing – and in those cases they'll typically report to the VP of that unit.

For their part, the experienced data scientists must support the citizen data scientists in developing solutions that will eventually be implemented in production environments. The availability of resources and time will typically determine where the analytics and models are built. If the COE staff has the time and skills, then the COE should build the models. But if the

COE is fully engaged in other projects and the citizen data scientists have the required skills and tools, then in the interest of time, they should build the analytics and models. Even then, that work needs to be submitted to the COE for testing and validation before it can be moved into production.

Once the models have been validated in a test environment, they are ready to be put into production. This is where the rubber meets the road. The models are now inserted into the production systems and they begin working on live data, producing results that will change how the organization operates. If all goes well, the changes are verified as improving the business, and the models remain in production until it's time for an update or replacement. (In Chapter 2, we discussed why models must continually be updated or replaced.) Verifying the results as an improvement in business operations is a joint effort by the experienced data scientists in the COE and the teams in which their operations are being affected. Experienced data scientists will work with the team members in marketing, sales, logistics or other areas to compare past performance with the new results to ensure that everyone agrees that the new models are delivering improved operational results.

During this period, the citizen data scientists own the solution and must monitor it for its ongoing reliability and effectiveness. At some point, they may engage the COE for an entirely different business objective, or they might want to implement a completely new analytical approach to the solution that was just developed. The new approach might, for example, potentially produce superior results with increased speed and reliability than the existing technique. If so, then another project might be undertaken to test the new technique to investigate whether it does indeed confer a competitive advantage.

And so, it goes. The ongoing quest for better business results means that companies are always monitoring the performance of existing models and searching for new avenues for competitive advantage. It never ends and any success, although sweet, will likely only be fleeting.

THE COE IN ACTION

The fundamental purpose of the COE team is to build analytics for the organization. The team may be brought in at the direction of the CEO to tackle a problem that has vexed others in the company, or the project may be one that is new and of strategic importance. The quality of products coming from a factory might be declining, for example, or perhaps customer satisfaction is plummeting, causing increased customer churn. No matter what the project, if it's based on or leverages analytics, the CAO and COE should own the creation of a solution.

After the COE has had some initial successes in a number of strategic projects, then the peers of the CAO will typically begin requesting that the COE help solve business-unit specific problems. Examples of such projects might include uncovering inefficiencies in the supply chain, predicting the most effective marketing approaches, or recommending the best approaches for reducing theft or loss. The range of problems that can be solved by analytics is virtually boundless.

In many cases, the initial request to the COE will be general in nature — for example, "help us determine the effectiveness of our marketing programs." The COE team handles that vague request by, for instance, demonstrating that online search engine optimization (SEO) programs produce $5 of revenue for every $1 spent. In comparison, physical direct mail produces a greater or lesser return. That result is interesting and valuable in and of itself, but it will likely spawn additional questions to dig deeper into the SEO and direct-mail programs. That's typically the way that the analytics journey begins and progresses down paths to greater specificity, all leading to deeper insights.

Once the COE has demonstrated repeated success in building solutions for operational areas and business units, it's time to start building out the analytics capability of the broader organization. After an operational area has engaged the COE and a solution has proved to be fruitful, that business unit needs to prepare itself for the maintenance and ongoing operation of that analytical application. Specifically, the unit should hire and train analysts to be part of its operational team. These individuals will then collaborate and cooperate with the COE team to ensure that the initial success of the analytical application continues and is refined and extended to adjacent areas of the business. The overall goal is to build out the organizational awareness, orientation, and capabilities such that analytics becomes a core competency of the organization, much like lean manufacturing or Six Sigma.

We should note here that the COE and its staff need not be a centralized function. That is, staffers could work in different offices around the world. Of course, the co-location of team members does have its benefits, but many COEs are globally distributed and are able to work effectively by using a wide range of technologies to collaborate and remain in sync. At Cisco's analytics COE, for example, staffers are distributed around the globe and they use videoconferencing technology to collaborate on a daily basis.

Conclusion

You run a business, and you want it to be as successful as possible. One of the tools that you can employ is analytics. In the great majority of analytics projects, you'll see operational and margin improvement. In most cases, you'll see an immediate return that will grow over time, more than paying for your investment. With analytics, your operations will improve across the organization and around the world, driving your company toward leadership in the areas that you designate.

Success, however, requires more than just sophisticated technologies. It also requires strong leadership and the right team. Indeed, every organization that we've been involved with that has obtained significant analytical results has had a small handful of capable and driven people who have believed in the technology and have driven the organization toward success. Moreover, without the commitment of the senior leadership (including the CEO), the analytics COE can lose funding and support over time and, when that happens, the commitment to analytics will dissipate – along with the organization's analytics talent.

As we have noted before, analytics paves a path to steady and consistent operational improvement and competitive advantage, but it is one that requires time, investment, and commitment. Without those, there's no long-term market advantage to be gained. Who knows how analytics COEs will evolve in the future? It's clear that without visionary and technically capable leadership, analytics will not prosper in an organization, and the resultant technology will fail to deliver the desired results.

CHAPTER 6
Getting Started

"The journey of a thousand miles begins with one step." – Lao Tzu

The Progressive Group of Insurance Cos. is at the cutting edge of advanced analytics. Through the use of transponder devices that people install on their vehicles, the company is able to track customers' mileage, the times of day they tend to drive, and their braking habits. That data enables Progressive to determine more accurate pricing, including which customers should and shouldn't receive insurance premium discounts (and the size of those discounts).

The system, called Snapshot, also provides tips to customers who want to improve their driving skills, and a user-friendly interface enables them to share their experiences on social networks.[1] Moreover, by analyzing the cumulative Snapshot data over the years (a total of more than 12 billion miles of driving), Progressive has been able to derive a number of key insights. It has found, for example, that hard braking is one of the most important variables for predicting future crashes, and that the safest drivers tend to allow an average of nearly a third more distance to stop.[1,3]

Building that kind of sophisticated analytics capability takes considerable time and resources. After all, as that well-known adage goes, Rome wasn't built in a day. That said, the right plan of action can help your organization slowly but steadily develop its analytics capability over time. In this chapter, our objective is to demystify that process.

BUILD OR BUY?

Generally speaking, the computer industry tends to advance in cycles that operate in a predictable manner. Novel functions are built into firmware – software that's permanently programmed into the memory of hardware. The hardware might be chips that are either application-specific integrated circuits (ASICs) or field-programmable gate arrays (FPGAs). These chips are manufactured in a fabrication plant and delivered to the customer ready to have new code loaded into them. Once the firmware is loaded, it lives and runs on the chip. The technology is a very fast method for executing code. In the database field, a wide range of companies have built such hardware-based systems and, in doing so, they were able to move the state of the art forward in dramatic fashion. Some of these early innovators included Teradata, Britton Lee, Netezza, and White Cross Systems.

Over time, the new functions (or sets of functionalities) evolve and are eventually built into widely available computer languages, such as C, Java, Python, and so on. From there, the functions can be programmed into infrastructure software (for example, for databases or networking) and application software (for example, for customer relationship management, logistics, or analytical platforms). Most business executives and managers might not be aware that the systems that they evaluate and buy today started out as combinations of hardware and software. For example, before Oracle and Sybase were available as software-based products, the only way to obtain a database was to buy a system that consisted of hardware and software from the vendors listed above.

From your viewpoint (and that of your team), the early adoption of a technology will have a number of important implications. If your organization has a compelling need for the latest innovative functions (the fastest databases, the most secure firewalls, and so on), then the solution might require an "appliance" (that is, hardware with permanent software) that can be deployed in your data center or cloud environments. For these types of systems, you will almost definitely be making a buy decision, because it's highly unlikely that you would be building this type of solution. In fact, we have not heard of even the largest commercial organizations, such as consumer and investment banks, logistics companies, and retail companies, building their own hardware appliances.

As new functionality is built into widely available computer languages, your options start to broaden. This is where you will need to look at the technical capabilities of your organization as well as its interest and appetite for incorporating innovative functionality into your systems based on the building blocks available in the market. How much of an investment is your company willing to make to develop a unique set of functions or systems that differentiate your operations and organization from the market?

When assessing the continuum from buy to build, you should consider the following: the more you buy, the more your systems, operations, and organization will be similar to everyone else's. On the other hand, the more you invest and build, the more differentiated your systems, operations, and organization will be from other firms in your market. Buying, building, and a blend of both can all be effective paths to take; it's just a matter of determining what will work best for your timeline, available resources, investment capability, and business objectives.

Of course, computers and the applications that run on them will continue to evolve, as the industry is perpetually developing a wide range of improvements and innovations. The process is ongoing, never ending, and exciting for those of us who have watched the progression of these technologies over decades. Currently, many of the top vendors have been working on a number of innovative improvements to analytic environments.

One such improvement has been an increase in the access to a wide range and quantity of globally dispersed information and raw data. In healthcare, for example, if a system has access to diagnostic codes, disease descriptions, diagnoses, patient information, and other various data, it can analyze all that input and quickly present to a doctor a ranked list of the likely diseases, potential complications, and most effective treatments. The potential here to improve healthcare is immense, but the challenge is to make the technologies both widely accessible and profitable for the companies that might invest to develop and build them. The legal industry also seems ripe for similar advances. Imagine a system that could sift through huge amounts of case law and statutes to a key precedent that was entirely relative to the legal issue at hand.

When you and your team are thinking about how best to leverage analytics for your organization, keep the following points in mind.

First, big data can be extremely useful. Of course, having years of data about sales and other types of transactions can be very valuable, no doubt. But it's not just the *volume* of data that's important. In fact, having a *variety* of data can be even more valuable. Data variety brings new perspectives to the analyses. As an example, in many cases when analyzing customer data only demographic and transactional data from one channel is employed. The analysis would be much improved if psychographic data and transactional data from multiple channels were included in the analytical processes. Sources for such data can be internal or external, proprietary or public.

Second, the majority of leading-edge analytical systems have eschewed the traditional method of analyzing data. The traditional approach is to clean the data, amass it in a centralized or local database, build predefined queries that run on the data, and provide the complete system to a defined set of users. As we've discussed earlier, that process is slow, expensive, error prone, and labor intensive. To be clear, there are numerous uses for the traditional approach outlined above, and many very valuable systems have been built this way. But this book is about advanced analytics, and advanced analytics calls for a new approach: to build systems that interface with a wide range of broadly (globally) dispersed repositories and sources of data. These distributed architectures have recently been made possible because of advances in high-speed connectivity, application programming interfaces (APIs), and other technological innovations. You and your team should be thinking about how best to bring together a wide range of data sources to deliver customer insights, learn more about manufacturing operations, optimize processes, improve sales conversion rates, cut costs, and so on. There is almost no area of your business that cannot benefit from such a distributed approach to advanced analytics.

Third, a crucial issue that's often overlooked is the ways in which users will interact with these new types of systems. In many cases, the new applications will be accessing data from widely distributed sources, and each of those subsystems may have significant information processing and computational tasks to perform to achieve the overall analytical objective. Moreover, your use cases may require the building of these subsystems that work in the background and do not have visible interfaces to the end users. Remember, as we've noted before, the most impressive and practical systems are those that are invisible. People do not necessarily need to know that advanced analytics is helping them make better decisions. After all, they'd much rather take full credit for their improved decision making without being constantly reminded of the help they're receiving!

CRUCIAL USER INTERFACES

In our experience, user interfaces can often make or break a system. The best applications will have a variety of output formats – narrative, graphical, tabular, voice, animation, and so on – with an easy-to-use interface. Beyond compelling visual interfaces and systems with speech recognition, systems are being designed today so that the operations they perform are intuitive to professionals in various fields, including doctors, nurses, and lawyers. In the past, systems have typically been developed by computer scientists who have not done a very good job of building interfaces for the wider population. Now, designers are a part of the process, resulting in greatly improved, compelling interfaces. Now interfaces present comprehendible information in work locations where professionals have access to those systems and can engage with them when they need assistance.

Consider the medical profession. Doctors, nurses, and other healthcare professionals often need access to analytic systems in real time. When they are faced with a challenging case or a difficult problem, they do not have the time or the luxury to stroll to a designated office where a special system is waiting for them. They need the system to be where they are, and accessible in a form that does not take them away from the situation they are immersed in. The system needs to be ubiquitous and always available to them when they choose to engage with it, and the interface has to provide them with the information they need efficiently and without subjecting them to cumbersome steps.

That's the goal of a prototype system being developed for the early detection of sepsis. A serious medical condition, sepsis occurs when a patient's body tries to fight an infection by releasing chemicals into the bloodstream that result in inflammation throughout the body, potentially leading to the failure of important organs. More than a million people in the United States suffer severe sepsis every year.[2,4] This particular prototype system is being developed by Hitachi Consulting, Vital Connect, and ClearStory Data. It relies on a patch that's worn on a patient's chest; sensors in the patch monitor the patient's vital signs, physical activity, posture, and any falls. The patch transmits that data wirelessly to a smartphone, where an app displays various information like heart rate, breathing condition, and skin temperature. In turn, the smartphone relays that data to a cloud repository that contains existing patient information from a variety of sources, enabling an analytic system to predict the likelihood of sepsis. When a particular individual's posture changes and his walking pace begins to slow (two signs of sepsis), for example, the system might then alert that person's healthcare providers to the increased risk.[2]

To emphasize a point that was made earlier, the best systems are invisible, like electricity. We don't think about the electrical power grid; we just know where the light switches are. That's how analytical systems should function. When we want to find the best movie to see, or identify the optimum routing for a particular delivery, or determine the best course of treatment, we would like to be able to engage with a system from the palm of our hand or through a voice-activated interface in our home, office, or car. Ideally, the analytics will deliver a solution seamlessly without our even having noticed.

THE MONETIZATION OF DATA

So far, we've focused on buying or building analytical systems that will make your business become more competitive, but there's another path to increased value. Companies like IBM, Altisource, General Electric, and many others have recognized that the data they hold in various operational systems is of great value not only to themselves but also to their customers and partners. Indeed, the mandate for many chief data officers (CDOs) is to make their organization's internal datasets available, accessible, and useful to internal and external groups. To that end, the short-term goal is to clean and catalog the data, and build the necessary infrastructure to monetize that information. The-long term objective is to convert the data operations from a cost center into a profit maker.

Already, a number of industries have established data-sharing agreements, some of which go back a number of years. Take, for example, Information Resources Inc. (IRI) and the Nielsen

Corp. (formerly AC Nielsen). Both firms rely on data-sharing agreements in advertising, merchandising, and sales in the consumer packaged goods (CPG) industry. Similarly, FICO and Experian exist due to data aggregation and information sharing in the financial services markets. Another example is the insurance industry, which now uses comparative rating software that's based on the pricing information pooled by insurance providers.

There's no reason why all industries couldn't benefit from building analytical applications that utilize widely dispersed datasets from a range of the major players in the market. In concept, benchmarking information for use in comparing processes across and within organizations is simple and easy to do – once people have access, of course, to the anonymized data from each participating firm and department. In practice, however, this has been difficult to accomplish across companies.

To date, the most progress being made in the area of data monetization is within firms. Altisource is a great example. The company has copious data from the entire mortgage process: the application, evaluation, approval (or denial), servicing, selling (and transferring to another firm), foreclosing, and closing of mortgages in different cities, counties, and states. With this wide range of data documenting the entire lifecycle of a mortgage, Altisource has been able to build various data products that cater to Wall Street, property managers, lenders, and other parties in the mortgage, housing, and related industries.

CONSIDER. THINK. DECIDE.

We have laid out what we've learned from decades of working in the analytics industry. Much of what we've written is based on solid case studies and real-world experience from organizations around the world in a wide range of industries. That said, we're almost certain that you'll have your own ideas of the current capacities and capabilities of your organization and staff, and the possibility of embarking on and sustaining a long-term journey in analytics. You may have nascent ideas of where you might want to take your organization on that journey. You might decide on having your organization embark on an enterprise-wide analytics journey that results in constant improvement over the long haul, or you may find that the better course of action is simply to improve isolated areas of your operations. Perhaps even a simple, localized project might make the most sense for your company.

A critical step at this juncture is to take the time to think about your organization and team, and ask yourself a number of key questions. Does my senior leadership value change, strive for improvement, and encourage curiosity from teams and their team leaders? Does my extended team work on an ongoing basis to experiment and to improve operations, products, services, profitability, and the experience of our customers, partners, and employees? Do we have the necessary attitude, will, and desire to undertake an analytics journey that will drive our business to higher levels of effectiveness, efficiency, and competitiveness? Can analytics help us to disrupt the status quo in our industry?

After thoughtful consideration of the above questions, you can then begin devising a plan to move forward. The decision to transform your organization into an analytically-driven continuous improvement engine should not be taken lightly. It will not be a short-term initiative, and it will not be an inexpensive proposition. The path will be long, requiring significant time, investment, resources (including the right staffing), organizational design, and - perhaps most importantly of all - fortitude.

It's often been said that "culture eats strategy," and the relevance of that saying is clearly evident here. If your culture is not receptive to analytics and continuous improvement, you may be better off to start with contained and controlled projects to see how the team and company reacts. There are numerous consultancies, technologies, service-based offerings, and vertical solutions that can help you scope a project to undertake a controlled experiment to see how your organization will react to this type of approach.

A HYPOTHETICAL PROJECT

We've talked at length about the different technical and organizational factors that companies should consider before implementing advanced analytics. Let's now walk through a hypothetical project, in which you and your team have decided to experiment with analytics for the logistics operation of your business.

Your direct report, the leader in the supply-chain area, is on board with the initiative and the logistic team seems engaged and ready. The senior leadership has decided that your team will work with a boutique consultancy that has a track record of success in implementing data analytic improvements in the logistics area. With goals that are well-defined, understood, and achievable, the project kicks off with enthusiasm from the internal team and the vendor.

Five weeks later, though, the project seems to have gone pear-shaped. Progress has been slow, and the schedule has slipped with several missed deadlines. The work continues to limp along for another five weeks, even while people's enthusiasm begins to wane and nothing seems to really be getting done. On the surface, reports are being written and meetings are being held, but concerning real progress toward the initial goals, the project is effectively D.O.A. What happened?

As it turned out, you and your business-unit leader were on-board, but the logistics team did not see the value of the project. Those staffers already thought that they were best in class, and they considered the analytics initiative as more of a nuisance than anything else. So they slowly but surely resisted the project in passive-aggressive ways. No buy-in, no success.

This, of course, was hardly the result you were hoping for, but a 10-week project is a relatively small investment to make in order to gain valuable insights into how your frontline teams might view these types of top-down initiatives. But the question must be asked: how could you have done a better job in getting everyone on board?

A team meeting in the core operational area is usually a good place to start. The discussion will enable you to gauge where people view their current efforts. Through that conversation, you could have learned that the team felt that it had already attained market-leading performance. Your next step would then have been to share case studies and examples of how companies in various industries (especially yours) have been achieving better performance than your organization. You and others could have then formulated a team challenge with rewards and incentives for increasing levels of effectiveness and efficiency.

It's important here to note that you might consider ways in which to convert this kickoff project into an ongoing effort or focus on continuous improvement. Of course, it's good to raise the bar and bring your organization up to the performance of market leaders. It's even better to steer your team away from a short-term perspective and toward the concerted long-term objective of attaining and maintaining a level of improvement that will differentiate your business in the market.

One of the benefits of a long-term orientation is that it requires a commitment from your organization to invest in a frontline team. The individuals on that team must have the necessary education, training, technology, and support. To achieve continuous improvement, the entire team needs to continually raise its game. Ideally, the analytic projects undertaken will engage those employees to learn new skills, driving them toward objectives (and incentives) that are good for them as individuals, instead of feeling obligated to do work that benefits only the company. Furthermore, the analytic initiative should foster a culture of change in the organization. It should not be just a pet project of the CEO or upper management, but an enterprise-wide imperative of organizational value.

Personally, we'd prefer short-term high-intensity projects, but we have seen far too many of them go off the rails, stretching past their deadlines and taking a toll on the best employees. If analytics and continuous improvement are what you seek, it's better to build these pillars slowly, in a focused and determined manner. Think "marathon" instead of "sprint."

Of course, there will likely be numerous setbacks along the way, and management must be prepared to continue providing support even when experiments fail. That support might include training classes from world-class experts, visits to complementary firms to learn what those businesses are doing, and investments in relevant systems, technologies, and process techniques.

For its part, the frontline or core team in the operational area chosen will need to collaborate with variations and combinations of both internal and external parties. Working with the IT team, for example, will be important for gaining access to data, hardware, software, and knowledge with respect to data wrangling and related technology-oriented topics. In addition, internal data scientists can help the core team understand the data available, the transformations needed, and the analytical techniques and best practices necessary for building analytics. Other important resources might come from the outside, such as external data scientists who might be interested in collaborating with your team as hired experts.

Once you have an internal group that's been successful, you will then have a SWAT or "tiger" team of evangelists. Success in one operational area can now be transplanted into new areas. The investments in people, processes, training, and technology will pay off as your internal sponsors are sent to other operational areas to spread the word about the company's new mode of operating.

Sometime during this process - perhaps when a second operational area is beginning to undergo the transformation to analytics - you and the senior leadership might begin discussing the possibility of creating an analytics center of excellence (COE). This COE, headed by a chief analytics officer (CAO), would drive the larger transformation of the corporation. In Chapter 5 we discussed the COE and CAO in the context of the larger organization, and in Chapter 3 we talked about the importance of the algorithm economy. The simple fact is that the future success of your organization's analytic capability will be less about the data and more about algorithms.

The bottom line is this: those companies that become the sources of innovative algorithms delivered in smart, effective, and seamless ways will find themselves in an enviable position to exploit market opportunities in ways that their non-analytic competitors will have great difficulty doing.

CONCLUSION

As we mentioned in the introduction to this chapter, Rome wasn't built in a single day; neither will your analytic capabilities be attained so quickly. That said, we have personally seen hundreds of companies begin their analytic journeys and gradually make significant progress toward greater competitive advantage. Of course, those journeys were not without their fair share of stumbles along the way. In our experience, success typically comes to those projects that have solid support from the top, that have marshaled the necessary resources, and that have done the required groundwork to prepare the organization for the upcoming changes. In Chapter 6, we discuss the typical problems that tend to derail these types of projects, and we provide advice for avoiding the common pitfalls.

Endnotes:

[1] Mary K. Pratt, "How Progressive Uses Telematics and Analytics to Price Car Insurance," CIO Magazine (July 26, 2013), available at http://bit.ly/2t0oUUk.

[2] Greg S. Martin, Sepsis, severe sepsis and septic shock: changes in incidence, pathogens and outcomes. US National Library of Medicine, April 1 2013 http://bit.ly/2topPkr.

[3] "Lead Foot Report from Progressive Insurance Busts Industry Braking Standards," Progressive Group of Insurance Companies, available at http://pgrs.in/2smcaVX.

[4] Thor Olavsrud, "How Big Data Analytics Help Hospitals Stop a Killer," CIO Magazine (July 17, 2015), available at http://bit.ly/1HAK2lp.

CHAPTER 7
Operational Analytics: Advanced Analytics in the Modern Corporation

"Action may not always bring happiness, but there is no happiness without action." – Benjamin Disraeli

We expect that the readers of this book are executives who are running companies in a wide range of industries and geographies around the world. Some of you may be in general management while others might be focused on specific functional areas. This chapter provides an overview of various functional areas and the ways in which we've seen companies use advanced analytics to improve those operations. The functional areas are presented in the order in which we've seen the greatest amount of return and highest number of implementations.

MARKETING/SALES

In modern corporations, the marketing department has typically been the primary home of advanced analytics. Once analytics and math techniques were developed and proven in a commercial setting, it didn't take marketing teams long to realize the value of that technology for their work.

The consumer packaged goods (CPG) or fast moving consumer goods (FMCG) firms were the first to begin to experiment with data analytics, with other companies following their lead. Companies wanted to use the technology to improve their efforts in marketing – not just to consumers, but also to customers of all types, including other businesses. (Note: For our purposes, we are using the broadest possible definition of marketing to include the following: mobile, direct, online, all disciplines of advertising, customer relationship management [CRM], pricing, personalization, content management, and more.)

Currently, marketing and sales departments are using advanced analytics for many different functions, including:

- To acquire new customers and retain existing ones

- To identify the most profitable customers and product opportunities

- To learn from previous transactions of how to structure prices, offers, products, and messages

- To refine cross-selling, upselling, and other sales techniques

- To determine the best times and channels to make specific offers

- To calculate the best physical locations for new stores

and many more. In fact, companies like Amazon have deployed advanced analytics to optimize virtually every aspect of its marketing, and those efforts have led to a number of invaluable insights. For example, Amazon discovered that even small delays in the time it takes consumers to load a webpage can lead to a significant drop in sales. Specifically, an additional wait of just 100 milliseconds could lead to a 1 percent decrease in sales.[1]

Another key lesson that Amazon has learned is the power of customer personalization. Years ago, many websites (including Amazon's) made frequent errors in personalization. When a consumer bought a book about Brahms' symphonies for a friend, for instance, he would later be bombarded with offers for books and CDs on Tchaikovsky, Schuman, and Chopin – even though he himself might have little interest in classical music. Today, models and data analytics have moved well beyond those early ham-handed approaches and can recognize when a purchase is an outlier versus when it's part of a pattern of previous behavior.

Indeed, current state-of-the-art systems are much more sophisticated in determining when and how to present cross- and upsell offers, and real-time analytics enable marketers to operate at the speed of business to interact with each customer in a tailored and customized manner. After all, consumers in Tokyo are vastly different than those in Houston, and having accurate analytic models that operate in real time, all the time, enables marketers to treat customers in the manner they desire – and have come to expect.

Clearly, marketing teams that employ advanced analytics can provide more compelling buying experiences at lower price points, which is more engaging and attractive to their customers. As such, their companies will grow more quickly and gain greater market shares. In industry after industry, analytics is at the core of the marketing operations of the majority of the market leaders. Amazon has gone all-in with respect to analytics. To compete with expert marketers like that online retail giant, firms in all markets will likewise need to make the necessary investments in their analytics capabilities.

FINANCIAL SERVICES

Like the marketing and sales function, the financial operations of a company can also benefit greatly from the use of advanced analytics. As it turns out, very sophisticated tools and techniques in this area have already been developed by the financial services industry. Consider just one function of the finance department of many companies: assessing the credit-worthiness of customers.

The granting of credit in the consumer, industrial, institutional, and governmental environments is a crucial part of the global economy. All players in these markets need to understand the risks that they are undertaking, as well as the financial profiles and histories of the entities to whom they are considering offering credit-based deals. Every organization that grants credit to another party must have a threshold or limit at which they draw the line on risk. For automobile loans, that threshold could be based on a person's credit history or credit score, income level, and a mix of other relevant factors. If a company can build better analytical models and refresh them with greater frequency to more accurately calculate risks and set the optimal thresholds, then it can gain a significant advantage over other organizations that lack that capacity. A firm could, for example, grant credit to customers that competitors might turn down, enabling it to grow its market share. It could also minimize the number and size of its delinquent payments and defaults, leading to increased profits.

One company that has become very proficient in doing so is Danske Bank, a leading financial institution in northern Europe. Thanks to advanced analytics, Danske is able to respond quickly to loan applications, not simply with a denial or approval but with specific credit limits. The models used to make those decisions are updated regularly with the availability of a variety of new data. This data is gleaned not just from customers, but also from external sources such as credit bureaus. Advanced analytics also enables Danske Bank to find patterns in that data, allowing the company to better predict whether a particular loan application will default within a year.[2]

Obviously, such techniques could easily be deployed by the finance departments of many corporations. Retailers could use them to better assess their risk in granting credit to consumers. Business-to-business (B2B) firms could deploy advanced analytics to calculate the credit worthiness of their corporate clients and the financial stability of their potential suppliers and partners. Furthermore, the technology could also be used in other, increasingly sophisticated ways.

Consider EOS KSI, a debt collector based in the Czech Republic. Collecting debts can be tricky for any business. If a company manages its accounts receivable department too aggressively, it could lose potentially valuable customers. On the other hand, if it allows too many of its customers to become delinquent, it could become unprofitable. EOS uses advanced analytics to strike the right balance. Thanks to copious data from past-due accounts, EOS can identify which debts are most likely to be collected, and which will probably be a waste of time trying to pursue. The company is also able to determine the most opportune time and method for seeking payments – for example, a phone call versus a letter that simply states the customer is overdue. Thanks to such advanced analytics and the corresponding automation, EOS has been able to reduce the time it spends on administrative tasks by 70 percent.[3]

We expect that the chief financial officers (CFOs) and finance departments of many corporations will increasingly use advanced analytics in the future. Some will take their lead from the financial services industry and Wall Street, where firms have been pushing the analytical envelope for years. Program trading, for example, has now become widespread and operates in every market around the world. In these applications, the models and platforms are set up to look for anomalies in markets and prices in every asset class and subclass. When anomalies or opportunities are detected, the programs take action to profit from those misalignments. No human can scan, detect, and act at the speed of these applications. Companies in every industry could also benefit from them, for instance, in handling the currency exchanges for their overseas operations.

LOGISTICS/SUPPLY CHAIN

As the world becomes more interconnected, there's an increasing need for companies to flexibly plan, execute, and reconfigure the processes, methods, and means of moving raw materials, works in process, finished goods, people, animals, packages, and other cargo from one place to another. In the

United States, companies like Frito-Lay and Coca-Cola have built competitive differentiation into their direct-to-store delivery systems, which helps them ensure prime placement and shelf space in stores. In the 70s and 80s, direct-to-store delivery systems were augmented with descriptive analytics; at the time, they were considered quite complex and advanced.

Today, the bounds of this technology have been extended and refined considerably, with companies like FedEx and UPS demonstrating on a daily basis the sophistication of logistics operations. These systems have taken logistics to an entirely new level. Instead of making deliveries to a handful of stores in each town, they now must accommodate every single address as a potential delivery point, and each day brings a new set of pickup and delivery points. Instead of having to optimize a route that is relatively static, the advanced analytics must deal with dynamic routes, with pickup and delivery points that might be continually changing throughout the day.

In the UPS system, called On-Road Integrated Optimization and Navigation (ORION), advanced analytics crunch data from a variety of sources (including GPS tracking devices on the delivery vehicles) to optimize a driver's route with respect to distance, fuel consumption, and time. ORION takes into account a variety of factors such as number of stops, start time, commit time, pick-up windows, and any special customer requirements.

Although UPS hasn't finished deploying the system to all of its more than 50,000 routes in North America, the results have already been impressive. According to the company, ORION has helped save more than 1.5 million gallons of fuel and reduce carbon dioxide emissions by 14,000 metric tons. If all goes well, the full rollout of the system will lead to even more dramatic reductions. Even a decrease of just one mile per day per driver would amount to an annual savings of up to $50 million.[4]

Although today's global logistics systems are quite advanced, there's still significant room for improvement. Today people working in the logistics field have been incorporating weather data, calendar information about events that might affect traffic, construction schedules, and more into their analytics models. The goal is to take into account all local and systemic factors that could have an impact on moving goods to their desired destinations. Given the room for improvement and the opportunity for outsourcing, we expect to see new firms redefining the logistics landscape in the coming years.

It's not just companies like UPS and FedEx that have been working on advanced logistics systems. Recently, Amazon realized that it would need to augment the capacity of both UPS and FedEx with its own in-house capability. This has led to a fleet of nondescript white vans with magnetic Amazon logos slapped on the side driving around neighborhoods making deliveries. Of course, few companies have the scale and resources to do what Amazon is doing, but that doesn't mean they can't benefit from the use of advanced analytics to improve their operational logistics. One area where many firms have had success is their supply chain management.

Take, for example, FLIR Systems, which designs, tests, and manufactures equipment for detecting chemical, biological, explosive, and other threats. There's little margin for error for FLIR's products. Any device malfunction could have huge repercussions, such letting a terrorist threat go undetected or triggering a false alarm that causes unnecessary panic. Accordingly, quality control is a very serious matter at FLIR.

The problem is that the company must rely on parts from various suppliers. Even slight variations in the quality of those items can have huge consequences. So, to help better manage its supply chain and increase its manufacturing productivity, the company implemented advanced analytics in one of its business units that manufactures handheld devices designed to detect trace levels of explosives. The new system monitors incoming parts and catches problems early on by analyzing streams of data from up to four or five different systems. That data has also enabled FLIR to better understand the key drivers of its production process, enabling workers to make important adjustments. The overall result has been that the company is now better able to avoid lengthy manufacturing shutdowns that, in the past, might have taken months to address. The result: a drop in product revenue losses of about 30 percent.

MANUFACTURING

Process and discrete manufacturing are often lumped together, but they are quite different operationally. The one common element they share, though, is the use of advanced analytics to improve the quality of the output.

PROCESS MANUFACTURING

Perhaps nowhere is the need for quality control greater than in the pharmaceutical industry. Biologic drugs are typically produced in large vats or vessels, and the process is similar to brewing at home. Materials are added to a vat, where active ingredients help build up or break down the desired compounds, which eventually become the drugs designed to treat a condition. Because the distilling or brewing processes can go awry at any time, it must be monitored closely. This typically involves more than just checking a few variables like temperature. Instead, what's required is to sample, distill, analyze, and then quickly determine whether an intervention is needed.

Moreover, if an intervention is indeed necessary, people must have specific information about the type of corrective measure that will bring the process back into the acceptable range while not overshooting the target. Without such measures in place, not only could thousands of gallons of product potentially be wasted, but also precious time could be lost. Many of these processes take months to complete, and patients might be relying on these batches for their health and happiness, if not for their very lives.

This is where advanced analytics has helped companies like Shire, a biopharmaceutical firm that provides treatments for gastrointestinal and rare diseases. Thanks to a sophisticated analytics system, Shire is able to spot manufacturing issues early on, and address them before they become larger problems that might potentially ruin a batch of product. The technology has enabled the firm to reduce the variability (and increase the predictability) of its production process, ultimately resulting in a decreased number of defects and fewer lost batches.[5]

Advanced analytics can also be used to replicate the best production runs. A major aluminum manufacturer, for example, has studied the factors that have contributed to high-yield months versus low-yield months. The company found that, on any given day, anywhere from 15 to 50 variables could affect the productivity of a production cell, and the variables could combine in thousands of ways. Interestingly, advanced analytics also enabled the aluminum maker to detect new variables that were affecting the smelting process.

Now the firm can continually monitor and adjust those key parameters, not only to improve productivity but also to reduce energy consumption. Furthermore, advanced analytics helps the company quickly deal with changes in a process parameter that's outside its control – for instance, an increase in the impurity concentration of a raw material used. By adjusting other variables, the process team can minimize the effects of such unexpected events. Thanks to those and other benefits, advanced analytics is saving the aluminum manufacturer millions of dollars a year.[5]

DISCRETE MANUFACTURING

Here, manufacturing is more about the assembling of pieces and parts instead of the distilling and refining of batch flows. In both cases, though, quality control has been the predominant reason for employing advanced analytics.

Discrete manufacturers must ensure that the parts being supplied to them for the assembly of their products are of the quality and reliability required. Advanced analytics can certainly be effective for that task, as we saw in the earlier discussion of FLIR Systems. In addition, the analytics system must also log and document the process flows, the types of models and the individual parts used, the timing of certain decisions, and other important information. Analyzing all that data helps FLIR make better decisions about its manufacturing operations. The company can, for example, determine quickly whether a particular anomaly is an issue that will likely correct itself versus one that will eventually become severe enough to cause a shutdown.

Obviously, product quality is a primary focus of analytics systems used in manufacturing, but that doesn't mean there aren't ancillary benefits. As mentioned earlier, FLIR has been able to reduce its product revenue losses by about 30 percent. Another company that has also achieved substantial cost savings thanks to the use of advanced analytics is

Instrumentation Laboratory, which manufactures medical devices and related technologies for blood and hemostasis testing. Every year, Instrumentation Laboratory manufactures hundreds of thousands of cartridges containing cards with sensors for measuring the electrical signals of blood that's being tested. Advanced analytics enables the company to quickly determine how changes in certain variables (like temperature and humidity) might be causing a particular issue. As a result, not only is the technology improving quality control at Instrumentation Laboratory, it's also helping to save hundreds of thousands of dollars by avoiding having to scrap batches of its cards during manufacturing.[6]

In the future, the analytics used in discrete manufacturing will provide even greater functionality. Already some forward-thinking manufacturers are working with their suppliers to connect and link their analytical systems. The potential benefits are considerable. Suppliers that are providing parts and work-in-process materials to downstream manufacturers often have varying tolerances for their many customers. A part or batch that may meet the standards of one customer might be rejected by another. By linking the analytical systems, the different batches can be routed in the most efficient ways to meet specific customer tolerances and quality levels. This will not only save the companies involved time, money, and resources, it will also reduce any rework.

Moreover, as manufacturing supply chains become integrated, it will be easier for the participating companies to look upstream into their supply chains and predict when a slowdown might be encountered – a major supplier might have, for example, suffered a shutdown at one of its largest plants. And if that upstream visibility is advanced enough, then mitigation plans can be implemented well before there's any shortage of parts or materials.

FRAUD AND THEFT

Every industry suffers from fraud and theft. Especially now, in our digital society with ubiquitous connectivity, mobile access, and demand for the convenience of easy-to-use apps for commercial transactions, companies have become increasingly vulnerable. To be sure, security systems and countermeasures have advanced dramatically in recent years. Specifically, firewalls, antivirus software, and multiple layers of validation and verification have made IT systems much more secure and, at the same time, more effective and efficient. Yet businesses still have much work to do with respect to securing their assets.

Indeed, according to a recent survey, only roughly one-third of security leaders have high confidence in their organization's ability to detect fraud and prevent any incursions from becoming serious problems.[7] In other words, companies need to find more effective ways to protect their operations, information, employees, customers, products, finances, and more. Advanced analytics can play a key role in closing this gap.

As discussed in Chapter 2, model portability was a significant step forward in the 1990s. That technology has continued to improve, potentially enabling analytics security systems to be adapted from one industry to another. Currently, the financial industry has developed some of the most sophisticated of such systems.

In today's fast-paced world of digital commerce, the real-time scoring of information in financial systems (credit card transactions, credit applications, and so on), marketing systems, fulfillment processes, special investigation units in the insurance industry, and other applications have been reducing losses by catching a higher percentage of all illicit activities. For banks, machine-learning algorithms have been helping to distinguish between those data anomalies that are innocent outliers versus those that indicate fraud. These types of analyses are being performed in real time, without any disturbance to the continuous, voluminous flow of legitimate transactions.

We are now seeing similar innovations in a wide range of industries. Indeed, companies of all types have been inserting advanced analytics into their processes, often alongside existing firewall and antivirus systems. The goal is to look at various transactional and behavioral patterns to detect and stop fraud, waste, and loss.

CONCLUSION

This chapter provided an overview of analytics systems that have been widely deployed in a range of functional areas: marketing/sales, financial services, logistics/supply chain, manufacturing, and fraud/theft.

Currently, various initiatives are being planned and implemented to advance the state of the art in each of these areas, as well as in many other functional departments not mentioned above, including R&D and human resources.

Our recent conversations with business leaders and senior managers in a number of industries indicate that many companies have already been expanding their capabilities considerably with respect to how data is acquired, managed, integrated, and exploited with advanced analytics throughout the different organizational functions. Indeed, in the words of the writer William Gibson, "The future is already here. It's just not very evenly distributed yet."[8]

Endnotes:

[1] Kit Eaton, "How One second could cost Amazon $1.6 Billion in Sales," Fast Company Magazine (March 15, 2012), available at http://bit.ly/1Beu9Ah.

[2] Statistica, "How Danske Bank improves Customer Service with Statistica," Dell Company Case study (November 12, 2016), available at http://bit.ly/2s1kMSG.

[3] Dell, "EOS KSI Česká Republika, s.r.o., simplifies credit analysis with Dell Statistica," Dell Customer Stories (March 2016), available at http://dell.to/2tXl92b.

[4] Jessica Lyons Hardcastle, "UPS Big Data to Cut Carbon Emissions, Save 1.5M Gallons of Fuel" Environmental Leader Magazine (October 31, 2013), available at http://bit.ly/2uhTmZD.

[5] Quest Software, "Shire: Specialty biopharmaceutical company reaps data analysis and process efficiencies" (March 2015), available at http://bit.ly/2tXBHab.

[6] Quest Software, "Aluminum maker crunches big data for top performance" (March 2017), available at http://bit.ly/2tkabFU.

[7] Kelly Bissell, Ryan LaSalle and Kevin Richards, "Accenture Security Index", (January 2017), available at https://accntu.re/2tkqLpP.

[8] WikiQuote, "William Gibson", (May 31 2017), available at http://bit.ly/2slJBIg.

CHAPTER 8
Analytics Everywhere, All the Time

*"Keep your eyes on the road and your hands upon
the wheel." – Jim Morrison*

The mining of precious metals and gems is a process that's rife
with inefficiencies and the potential for theft. To ensure
profitable operations, companies must control losses at every
stage. Even when processes are designed with the appropriate
number, type, and timing of checks and balances, advanced
analytics can add an additional layer of scrutiny and security.
That was the experience of one global corporation, a leader in
the operation of gold and diamond mines with a complex
network of sites that are offshore, deep underground, and in

some of the most remote places in the world, including the Arctic.

At the company, processes for ensuring the security of the extracted gold, diamonds, and other precious materials include providing employees with complete work uniforms that must be worn when entering and exiting work areas, and subjecting new personnel to multiple body scans and body inspections. Even the most careful and well-designed processes, though, aren't foolproof. That's where advanced analytics comes in.

By using the technology to analyze copious data from various sources – including surveillance devices at the mines – a loss-prevention team has been able to identify anomalies and exceptions in the processes. In one case, the team discovered that a small subset of employees had not been subject to a number of the more rigorous screening steps for an unusually long period of time.

Advanced analytics also helped uncover areas where workers could collaborate to circumvent certain processes. This finding led to an investigation that recovered a significant amount of material, leading to personnel reassignments and process redesigns. Overall, advanced analytics achieved its return on investment (ROI) in only about 14 months through the recovery of stolen products valued in the hundreds of thousands of dollars. The technology was also able to reduce high-risk process incidents by 25 percent.

AGILE AND UBIQUITOUS

In Chapter 5, we gained a solid sense of what a winning team looks like, and we learned how we should go about building that team. We also know the approach that we should take to solve a business challenge at hand. Now, we must understand the different ways to implement analytics to ensure our greatest probability of success.

In the past, analytics were implemented in a centralized, controlled environment. Imagine the stereotypical image of people with lab coats, working in a small office in an out-of-the-way corner of the corporate campus. Analytical solutions were implemented in an offline or batch mode, working on data that had been recorded after the fact. Because of that somewhat static environment, analytics professionals tended to implement solutions in the same way, batch oriented and with very little to no context of the real-world operations of the business, which didn't always lead to the best results. As the proverbial saying goes: when all you have is a hammer, then everything begins to look like a nail.

Today, analytics teams are young, distributed, and collaborative. The tools they use are fairly new and enable an agile approach to keep up with dynamic business conditions. Let's examine the various facets of how to implement an analytic solution given the new team structure, the macro environment, the available technologies, and the speed at which business is conducted.

REAL TIME

Customers and businesses are connected and interacting with each other on a 24 x 7 x 365 basis. Transactions are occurring continuously and constantly. This can be seen as a tremendous opportunity or an impossible challenge. In many markets, the leading companies are viewing it as the former and not the latter.

SPEED, MEASURED IN HOURS

In the past, companies would take months (if not years) to perfect an analytic model and implement it into a production system. Now, businesses can train models in a few hours on a substantial quantity and variety of data. Indeed, there are a number of well-known case studies in a range of industries in which models are being trained, vetted, and put into production systems on a daily basis.

Danske Bank has a well-refined process for building and deploying credit-risk models in half the time it used to take.[1] That capability has helped the firm gain market share and improve customer satisfaction without any increase in the default or delinquency rates. Ideally, companies want their analytic models to have reliability, accuracy, speed, and transparency (the ability to explain how a model works and why it improves business results). All that can be attained; don't let anyone tell you otherwise. Accomplishing it, however, typically requires a company to build automated training and testing systems to ensure that the breadth and depth of conditions are satisfied, and that the systems can be easily understood and reliably built.[1]

MODEL PORTABILITY

Previously, if a model was built using a platform like SAS or SPSS, it had to then run in one of those proprietary systems. Today, models can be built and converted into a wide range of languages, including R, Python, C, C++, Predictive Modeling Markup Language (PMML), Portable Format for Analytics (PFA), and Java. That is, if the systems a company runs are Java-based, its analytic teams can build, train, and test models in any environment that they prefer. Then, when a model is ready to go, it can be converted into Java code, verified, and placed into production. Over the years, model portability has been greatly enhanced by the ability to convert models into code that is optimized for a wide range of target platforms and by the creation of standards like PMML and PFA.

Model portability can be a godsend when a company grows by acquisitions or if it finds itself with multiple types of production platforms. Perhaps a firm's online transaction system is built in Ruby, its CRM system in C, and its survey system in Java. No problem. Assuming that one model will work across all three systems, the company can build, train, and test that model and convert it into Ruby, C, and Java, and then put all those variants into production.

Another huge advantage of model portability is that it frees a company to upgrade its technology to new vendors and approaches without worrying about being locked in. Remember years ago, when consumers wanted to change their cell phone carriers? They were assigned new phone numbers, and that inconvenience was a barrier to switching carriers. Today, consumers have local-number portability; people can keep their current cell phone number no matter what carrier they use in the future. Similarly, companies today don't necessarily have to scrap their existing library of models when they switch to a new language or platform.

MODELS EVERYWHERE

More than 30 years ago, companies could only build and run models in very tightly controlled and prescribed conditions. First, the environment had to be a data center or a lab where all the data had been careful cleaned and engineered. Second, it had to be a computing environment that had been architected to handle the data and computing complexity. Third, it had to be staffed with highly trained professionals who understood the algorithms, data, and type of results being produced. Fourth, it had to involve an analytical team that could interpret the results and apply them to the conceptual case being addressed. And fifth, it had to include business analysts who could work with the analytical team to extrapolate the results and apply them to a hypothetical business case.

A significant limitation of these models of the past was that they had to live in the data environment in which they were created. This meant that they were limited to theoretical applications or experiments. Thus, because a company had to extract the data from the source systems and bring it to the lab, there was no way that real-time operations were possible. This meant lengthy cycles for refreshing and revising models. Today, it's difficult for many people to believe that in the past we could not insert models into transactional systems. But that's how things were. It was either cost prohibitive or technologically impossible to recreate the complete data, training, and testing conditions in the transactional environment.

Innovations have since enabled us to transcend that limitation. As with most areas of computing, we have moved from those highly centralized and tightly controlled conditions to an environment that's globally distributed and loosely coupled. Inserting models into transactional systems is commonplace today; we'd be surprised if a major organization weren't currently using predictive models to monitor customer activity and behavior. Many consumers, for example, have become accustomed to calls, e-mails, and text messages from financial institutions (banks, credit card companies, and so on) asking them if they had executed a certain transaction that may have been outside their typical behavior. These alerts, for the most part, are the results of predictive models scoring our transactions in real time.

The majority of these models in production today are still being run in the cloud infrastructure or in corporations' data center environments. We are now beginning to see distributed models working in conjunction with other models. In these systems, the models all contribute their insights to provide an evenly distributed layer of real-time intelligence. This supports the smooth operations of a business while producing useful insights to enhance the customer experience, forestall outages, stop fraud and waste, and improve the effectiveness and efficiency of operations.

MOVING MODELS TO THE DATA

The newest innovation is for businesses to place the analytic models near the edge of a network. Indeed, models are now operating in real time in Internet of Things (IoT) gateways and other computing environments, all embedded at intermediate points and at the peripheries of networks. These models could be running in factories, retail stores, offices, homes, and many other locations.

For IoT environments, the amount of data generated can be immense. If a light bulb signals its status each second, it would create 86,400 data points in a single day. Think of how many light bulbs are in your office, company building, surrounding neighborhood, city, and so on. No network in the world could handle that volume of data. It's just not physically possible to move that kind of data to the cloud, a data center, or a local environment for analytical processing. Instead, what's required is the ability to move analytic models to the data, and that capability exists today.

Such "edge" models can be built for a variety of tasks. They can perform data reduction by looking for interesting patterns or deviations from the norm, and then only sending back alerts about the patterns themselves. They could also score data streams, looking for security anomalies, behavioral deviations, opportunities to cross-sell and upsell, chances to intervene to redirect online navigation, instances of automated redirection to a call center from an automated attendant, and so on. These "edge" models could also process images or streams of them, looking for indications of illicit activity (for example, the illegal streaming of movies) or of potential opportunities (for example, redirecting customers to products that are better suited to their needs).

With models reaching the edges of networks, we have entered the era of analytics ubiquity. Models are now running in the cloud, in our data centers, at the network locations just inside our firewalls, in local malls, in myriad gateways, and at the peripheries of networks of all types. These models are everywhere and they are working at all times, enabling business to modify data, redirect behaviors, cross-sell and upsell products, and do countless other things – all at the point of data generation.

Model monitoring and management. As models become ubiquitous, running all the time, how can we monitor, manage, and control them? Indeed, model management is one of the key challenges in making models everywhere a practical reality. Consider that we have reached the point where we can build, refresh, and revise models almost continuously. We can build systems that train and power neural networks. We can build heavyweight models that are immense in size and processing power. We can also build lightweight models that can be inserted into the smallest IoT gateways and sensors. We can do all of this, but if we cannot monitor, manage, and control these models, we will be limited in our ability to leverage the full value of that technology.

Fortunately, with the improvement of bandwidth and connectivity, we can now track, measure, and predict the need for a model to be refreshed or removed from service. Of course, firms would prefer to own their monitoring systems as company-based assets, but we nevertheless believe that the most valuable model monitoring systems will be cloud-based and will be run by third-party firms as a contracted service. In addition, we are now beginning to see advanced model management systems for refreshing a model or set of models according to preset thresholds and limits on drift and performance, which are crucial to ensuring the quality of those analytic systems.

LIMITED ONLY BY THE IMAGINATION

Companies that have met the above challenges are succeeding in a variety of applications in a range of industries. Indeed, these analytic systems seem limited only by the imagination. Let's take a look at a few of the more innovative applications we've seen so far:

ADP

When it comes to employment data, payroll giant ADP has perhaps the richest collection ever assembled. Through its 600,000 clients, ADP helps manage the payroll and other human resources (HR) information for 24 million employees in the United States. All that data is a digital treasure trove, and the company is now deploying advanced analytics to uncover valuable insights. For starters, ADP can supply benchmarking statistics across industries, so that clients can determine whether they might be under- or overpaying employees for various positions in different geographic locations. The application can also help spot certain trends – for example, are employees leaving primarily because they're unhappy with their salaries, their commutes, or some other factor within the organization? Moreover, ADP can help identify high performers who are likely to leave in the near future, thereby enabling their employers to take proactive and preventative measures.[2]

WHIRLPOOL

In an interesting IoT application, Whirlpool has been installing sensors in its appliances to ultimately improve the quality and lifespan of those products. The data collected includes information about the current state of the appliances as well as the usage patterns of consumers. By analyzing that data with machine-learning algorithms, Whirlpool can uncover valuable information for its R&D group. For example, a particular part of a washing machine might perform well for regular weekly washes but tend to break for consumers who do numerous loads concentrated throughout a single day, with long periods of inactivity separating those days. Using that information, Whirlpool could then redesign that part for future models.[3]

GEORGIA AQUARIUM

When tourists visit Atlanta, the Georgia Aquarium is typically among their "must see" attractions, and therein lies the problem. In the past, the aquarium would often become overcrowded, leaving visitors with a less-than-satisfactory experience. In fact, management discovered through customer feedback that the variable most highly correlated with visitors having a bad time was large crowds. This was a big concern because 90 percent of the aquarium's revenues came from ticket sales. So, management knew it had to get this issue right, and it turned to advanced analytics for a solution.

Figuring out the exact number of people who were in the facility at any given time was not as easy as it might seem.

Counting the people who had entered was simple because their tickets had to be scanned, but counting those who had left was tricky. The problem was that the exit turnstiles often broke, and many customers (especially the elderly and handicapped) would often leave through separate gates. The aquarium installed security cameras with image recognition to count the departing guests. Through an analysis, the aquarium discovered that the optimum attendance at any given time was around 4,500 people. (The official capacity of the facility is much higher than that, but 4,500 was deemed best for visitor comfort.)

Armed with that knowledge, the aquarium could adjust the online sales of its tickets, which customers purchased according to their planned time of entry. Of course, some people might stay at the aquarium only for an hour or so, while others might remain for five or six hours. The analysis found that the average was around three hours, but that figure depended on the time of day. Taking into account those and other variables, the aquarium could fine-tune the number of tickets it sold for every scheduled hour of every day it was open for business. The results were impressive. In 2014, the aquarium logged 60 days when there were more than 6,000 visitors in the building at any given time. In 2015, it had just two days when there were more than 5,000 people.

NASCAR

In auto racing, the difference between winning and losing can come down to fractions of a second, and the car tolerances to keep a vehicle running in tip-top shape are measured in the thousandths of an inch. Under such demanding conditions, advanced analytics can provide a significant competitive edge in crew performance during crucial pit stops. That's the goal of the Richard Childress Racing team, which has embedded sensors into its pit equipment to measure a host of variables, including the torque and positioning of the tire change process. Other sensors measure the reaction of a vehicle to the driving conditions, enabling the team to determine more effective racing strategies.[4]

CONCLUSION

The environments used to develop advanced analytics have changed dramatically in a number of important ways. We have moved from the era of the lone, brilliant research scientist to a widely-distributed team focused on communication, collaboration, and shared work. Also, we have moved from a time when most of the work performed was lost due to the ineffective nature of our communications systems, tools, and modes of operating to an era when our environments have transparency and daily engagement across all levels of the organization.

Furthermore, we have moved from tools that were the domain of PhDs and specialist statisticians to tools that enable business analysts and citizen data scientists to contribute their knowledge and creativity. We have moved from proprietary tools that had prohibitive price tags to open source tools and new languages that are specially developed to meet our needs in data management and in analytics.

We have moved from centralized environments housing rigid hardware and software that required significant effort to simply obtain the data needed to model a business operation to globally distributed, loosely coupled environments with high-speed network and access to data on a real-time basis. What's more, we have moved from the centralized scoring of data to moving models out to the edge of networks so that they can score, manage, and act on data in the same second that that data was created.

And what has been the end result of all these improvements? The answer, as we have seen in this chapter, is this: analytics everywhere, all the time.

Endnotes:

[1] "Bank Speeds Time to Market with Advanced Analytics," available at http://dell.to/2t0q0PP.

[2] Thor Olavsrud, "ADP Delivers Big Data Platform for Workforce Management Insights," CIO magazine (May 13, 2015), available at http://bit.ly/2tkswm6.

[3] Emily S., "Whirlpool: Are these the appliances of your dreams?," Technology & Operations Management at Harvard University (November 18, 2016), available at http://bit.ly/2s1H4no.

[4] Nicole Spector, "Here's What Brands Like Whirlpool and Nascar Are Learning From Internet of Things Data," Adweek (March 11, 2016), available at http://bit.ly/2t0JiF3.

Chapter 9
Innovative or Icky?

"For good ideas and true innovation, you need human interaction, conflict, argument, debate." –
Margaret Heffernan

How much do businesses know about us? When it comes to a company like Target, the answer is: quite a lot.[1] For many of its customers, the giant retailer knows their age, whether they're married, if they have children, where they live, their estimated salary, whether they've moved recently, what websites they may have visited, and so on. The company can also buy data to learn even more about its customers, including their ethnicity, their job history, the magazines they read, their political leanings, what they talk about online, and more.

All this information coupled with sophisticated analytics can be a powerful tool, enabling Target to determine, for example, when some of its customers might be pregnant. The company might then mail those women various coupons for maternity clothes, cribs, strollers, diapers, and other baby products.

Such marketing activities, however, might not be appreciated by everyone. In one case, a father in Minneapolis went to his local Target store to complain that his teenage daughter was receiving coupons for expectant mothers. "Are you trying to encourage her to get pregnant?" asked the irate father. Only later, after returning home, did the father discover that his high-school daughter was indeed already pregnant, leading to this somewhat unsettling headline in Forbes: "How Target Figured Out a Teen Girl Was Pregnant Before Her Father Did."[2]

Many consumers were none too happy to learn about how Target was deploying its advanced analytics capabilities. One commentator to the Forbes story noted the following: "Do we turn ourselves into East Germany circa 1970…except now we fear having coffee at Starbucks and paying with a credit card because of the date-and-time history and the tracking of what we bought and the video camera surveillance and your location history on your phone along with your friend's phone location."[3]

As Target and numerous other companies have learned, any innovation isn't without its consequences, and the field of data analytics is no exception. Of course, early adopters and some in the industry might marvel at the exciting new innovations and insights that are driven by data, but many people won't appreciate the elegant algorithms or clever applications. For them, a sophisticated system that knows when someone is pregnant before she may have told her family and friends is, well, just a bit creepy. This brings us to the golden rule of analytics: *just because you can, doesn't mean you should.*

PUSHING THE INNOVATION ENVELOPE

The acceptance of advanced analytics has been growing throughout society, becoming commonplace – and perhaps even expected – in many day-to-day interactions. But companies would do well to remember that people still need to be assured that their privacy and the data itself are being managed in a smart and organized way. As with most new technologies, regulation and governance tends to follow on the heels of innovation. That is, as we're able to do more sophisticated and interesting things with data and analytics, there will be a chorus of concern as people push back and demand control over these types of technologies. Of course, not everyone will have the same reaction. Many online shoppers might welcome having a retailer suggest products based on their past purchases, while others may find those recommendations to be invasive.

More than a century ago, as people were beginning to move from horse-driven carriages to automobiles, many had difficulty making the transition. To ease the discomfort of those consumers, some early autos had a fake horse head mounted in the front (see Figure 7.1). Today, that contraption may seem absurd, but companies should beware its lesson. People are generally wary and even afraid of change, and some will cling to the existing familiar. As such, pushing the adoption of new technologies forward can be a tricky endeavor, requiring companies to continually ask whether they might be pushing some customers too far beyond their comfort zones.

Given that the perception of end users, customers, and consumers can vary greatly, firms will find it difficult to identify boundaries when trying to determine how best to utilize data and advanced analytics. For businesses on the front line of innovation, executives must feel much like they're in a Star Trek episode, boldly going "where no man has gone before." But companies would do well to remember that the business world has many boundaries that the physical universe does not.

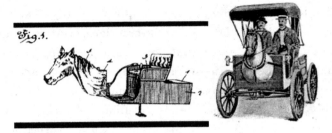

Figure 7.1.[4]

Over the years, sensitivities to privacy and data access concerns have been growing with every new report of a security breach at a major corporation like Sony, Neiman Marcus, Home Depot, or JP Morgan Chase. Target itself suffered a massive breach in 2013, when the personal information of millions of its customers was stolen.[5] Not surprisingly, such incidents have only intensified the public's cries for better compliance and stricter regulations.

To be sure, many companies could do better with respect to protecting the privacy of their customers. Some businesses may have indeed pushed the envelope too far when it comes to the use of analytics in marketing and other areas. In this chapter, we propose a three-part litmus test that executives can use to assess whether their latest ideas for innovative analytics might be inadvertently overstepping ethical bounds, and we then examine several examples with that test in mind.

Context, Permission, and Accuracy

We would be the first to admit that we are not experts on ethics or the legal issues involved with respect to data analytics. Based on our extensive business experience, though, we suggest that companies deploying the technology consider three important factors: **context, permission,** and **accuracy.** By taking into account all three factors, executives will be better able to gauge whether a particular application will be perceived as reasonable to the many stakeholders involved.

Context. Many people are perfectly fine with expert predictive analytics that improve customer service. When they visit a leading e-commerce site that's able to suggest "what else" they might like or predict the color of a garment that they might like best, they aren't put off by these types of insights into their buying habits, because the suggestions are contextually in line with the buying experience.

But consider the following example. Alice goes online to buy new knobs for her kitchen cabinets – literally a once-in-a-lifetime purchase for her. The internet, however, has a long memory. For weeks afterward, whenever Alice is online she continually receives ads for cabinet knobs, even from companies that she had long ago rejected. Other ads for cabinetry and countertops seem to assume that Alice is going to completely renovate her kitchen, which is not the case. Even when Alice is shopping online for totally unrelated products like books or laptop computers, she is still bombarded with those kitchen-related ads. For Alice, those ads are more than just irritating; they're invasive. The key issue with context is whether the use of advanced analytics is adding value to customers *without* infringing on their comfort level. In Alice's case, the kitchen-related ads failed both criteria.

Permission. Of course, consumers today are generally aware that businesses are harvesting information from every click they make on a webpage, from every product that goes into their online shopping cart, from the phone numbers that they dial, and so on. Many people, however, aren't knowledgeable of the full extent of the data-collection practices that many companies utilize, nor do they have a deep understanding of the sophisticated analytics involved. In many cases, permission is a relatively straightforward issue, and customers would gladly "opt in" to relinquish some of their privacy in exchange for certain benefits. Airline frequent-flyer programs are a classic example of that. In other cases, though, permission is a much trickier issue.

Consider cell phone plans. Few consumers take the time to read the privacy statement of the contracts they sign with their mobile company. If they did, they might learn that they've given their permission to have the phone numbers they dial logged and stored into a database. That information might then be used in ways that few consumers might have anticipated. If, for example, mobile Company A is aware of the fact that Bob called mobile Company B shortly after his having a service outage or after he's had a billing dispute with Company A, then Company A could then segment Bob as a "customer at risk." This could then set off multiple processes to retain Bob as a customer. Some of these processes might include discounts or even rebates that Bob might appreciate. But what if Bob has already made the decision to defect, but then he becomes pestered with aggressive calls from salespeople at Company A?

Strictly speaking, Bob did grant permission for Company A to collect and use his data, but did he truly understand what that might mean when he signed his contract? And if he somehow did read the tiny print of the long privacy statement that was buried deep in the contract, could he have anticipated that Company A would utilize his data in that way? Permission is indeed a complicated issue, but the lesson here is that permission with respect to contract law is one thing; the customer's perception of that permission can be quite a separate matter.

Accuracy. An online cartoon depicts a man turning away from his laptop to tell his coworker, "I think my Nest smoke alarm is going off. Google AdWords just pitched me a fire extinguisher and an offer for temporary housing."[1] Although funny, the cartoon does raise an interesting point. The analytics behind the Nest smoke alarm and Google AdWords may indeed be accurate in terms of predicting a disastrous fire, but the simple truth is that advanced analytics can also be imprecise and, in many cases, downright erroneous.

In practice, there are many use cases where "good enough" analytics are all that's required to deliver the value for a project. But when accuracy affects context or creates an environment in which actions can be affected by algorithms, it's critical to understand the technology's potential impact. Indeed, the lack of accuracy can place a company in a vulnerable position, subject to substantial financial losses and subsequent legal actions. (In Chapter 3, we discussed the disastrous case of Knight Capital, which managed to lose $440 million because of an application that lacked accuracy and the proper governing mechanisms.)

On the other hand, too much accuracy can also be an issue. Consider a hypothetical application that could accurately predict which married couples were going to divorce even before they themselves knew. Imagine those individuals receiving ads for divorce attorneys a few months before their marriages have actually hit the rocks. Yes, sometimes too much accuracy can be a downright creepy thing, especially when it invades a user's privacy and catches them totally off guard.

TARGET'S TARGETING OF PREGNANT WOMEN

Our three-factor litmus test – context, permission, and accuracy – can be helpful in assessing whether any particular application might lead to customer backlash. Let's return to the Target story.

Generally speaking, the technique of combining and analyzing multiple data sources to derive a new data point or piece of information isn't inherently controversial. For instance, meteorologists regularly take readings of many variables (temperature, humidity, barometric pressure, wind speed, and so on) from multiple sources. That data is then combined and analyzed using an advanced analytics platform to derive weather predictions. Society greatly benefits from those forecasts, especially when they accurately predict the arrival of hurricanes, blizzards, and other adverse weather events. In such cases, we are grateful for the advance warning and aren't particularly concerned about the intricacies of the underlying analytics used to make the prediction.

Target did something very similar. The company tasked an employee – Andrew Pole – with the job of increasing sales and margins in a particular area of their retail stores.[6] Pole brought together multiple sources of data that existed within the enterprise to better understand how customers were purchasing various SKUs. So how did Target figure out that some of its customers might be pregnant? As it turns out, an analysis of the data uncovered the interesting insight that pregnant women tend to buy unscented lotions around the beginning of their second trimester. They're also more prone to purchase calcium, magnesium, and zinc supplements. In fact, Pole and his advanced analytic system were able to identify about two dozen products that indicated which customers were most likely to be pregnant. The question then is: should Target have used those insights to send certain targeted customers unsolicited marketing materials?

Two issues are important here: permission and context. Women who sign up for Target's baby shower registry would likely not be offended to receive coupons for cribs, strollers, and other baby products. In fact, they might welcome those coupons and be grateful for them. Other women, though, could easily be offended to receive the same direct marketing mailings, which they might perceive as an invasion of their privacy and out of context of the relationship they thought they had with the retail giant.

People who have heard about the Target case have had a wide range of reactions, depending on their perspective. Some might applaud Target's use of advanced analytics as uniquely innovative, while others have criticized it as shockingly invasive. Your own viewpoint may be influenced by your age, your gender, and your regional location. Many people who live in the European Union (EU), for example, have been up in arms over the possibility of companies creating and using derived data. In fact, there's already legislation in place in the EU that would require companies to notify their customers when they are planning to sell derived data to a third party that didn't share the source data in the first place. This heated debate over the ownership of derived data will not likely be settled anytime soon, as it raises important questions about people's privacy.

ABOUT THOSE "FREE" DRINKS

Among the earliest adopters of advanced analytics were companies in the hospitality and entertainment industry, and many of those firms have become quite skilled in their use of loyalty programs, direct marketing strategies, and customer upgrades. Casinos in particular have pushed the innovation envelope in using their data to boost revenues. To that end, the membership or loyalty cards that casinos offer have been instrumental in implementing permission-based data collection. Those programs provide an effective mechanism to provide customers with offerings in an accurate and contextual way, with the goal of getting people to spend more time at a casino (and therefore more time gambling).

Consider the following hypothetical example. You walk into a casino and insert your loyalty card into a slot machine. The casino can now identify your presence and retrieve historical data on the length of time you tend to play, the type of machine you prefer, and the average amount of your bets. And, more importantly, the casino has information about when you tend to stop gambling based on your threshold for losses. So, for instance, if you're the type of player who sits down at a slot machine and is willing to lose $100, but after reaching that limit you generally move to a different activity or property, then a casino that utilizes analytics may try to find ways to intercede. Thus, as you approach your threshold of $100, a cocktail waitress may appear to offer you a free drink. If this has ever actually happened to you, then you know that the service concerning the free drink is never fast or expedient. Yes, the idea is to get you to make a commitment to the cocktail so that you feel compelled to wait for the waitress to return and, upon waiting, you're likely to put more money into the slot machine and continue gambling. Casinos are now moving to an electronic version of the same strategy, with new machines having the ability to alert you to the opportunity for a free drink, a complimentary meal, or some other bonus to entice you to stay.

Using the litmus test of context, permission, and accuracy, we might surmise that casinos are staying within the boundaries of propriety. If anything, though, this may be a case of too much accuracy. That is, we all might welcome a weather forecast that could accurately predict the path of a hurricane a week before it hits land. And we might be grateful for a medical diagnosis that alerts us to a potential health issue well before it becomes a fatal condition. But, at the same time, we might not always be appreciative of a machine that can accurately predict what we're planning to do and then take measures to undermine our actions.

THAT FEELING OF BEING WATCHED

Retailers have for a long time used data analytics to better understand who their customers are and what their purchasing behavior is like, with many companies at the leading edge of the technology. A boutique retailer, for example, has recently started using very expensive and beautiful mannequins designed and built in Italy. These mannequins are stationed throughout the boutique, one to the far left, one in the middle facing the door, and another off to the right facing the checkout area. These mannequins do their standard job of showing off the attractive clothes available in the boutique, but they also have an added function. Equipped with high-definition cameras behind their eyes, the mannequins collect data throughout the retail environment, and that information is then analyzed and used to improve business at the store.

Take, for example, the mannequin that faces the door. That mannequin keeps track of people as they walk back and forth in front of the store, taking into account how many people pass by and how many enter the store. From that data, management can determine whether certain window displays might be more effective in attracting customers. The mannequins can also track people as they move throughout the store, providing management with traffic patterns and dwell times that can be analyzed.

So far, none of this sounds like it might offend anyone, but here's where things get really interesting. The mannequins also utilize facial recognition software that enables the store to determine your gender and your general age group while you shop. Moreover, this particular retailer has the capability of matching up your face with your point-of-sale transaction (the time of the transaction and the credit or debit card used). The endgame for this retailer is a highly personalized shopping experience in which the store system will automatically identify you when you arrive (thanks to the facial recognition software), access your historical purchasing data, and feed information to sales associates on the floor so that they can better serve you.

Facial recognition software by itself isn't necessarily good or bad (although the analytics being considered by that boutique retailer might leave many people feeling somewhat uneasy). As it turns out, the technology has numerous applications beyond retail. For example, the company Faception[7] has developed a system that uses 15 proprietary classifiers of facial features to determine if an individual might be a terrorist or pedophile. The accuracy rate is reportedly 80 percent, and the recommendation is to use the software only as a starting point, from which additional sources of information can then be deployed to make a better determination.

Of course, it's one thing for a law enforcement agency to use facial recognition software to prevent crime; it's quite another for a clothing boutique to use similar technology to increase its sales. Returning to our three-factor litmus test, we believe that context and accuracy may not be a huge concern for that particular retail application, but shoppers might feel differently about the issue of permission.

FINDING THE RIGHT PATH

The example of that retail boutique provides a glimpse into how easy it is for a company to derive and use the personally identifiable information (PII) of customers in everyday transactions. Firms that deploy analytics will need to determine how derived data might fit into the goals, culture, and standards of their organization. Indeed, there's a fine balance that must be struck by companies wanting to utilize advanced analytics in their organizations (Figure 7.2).

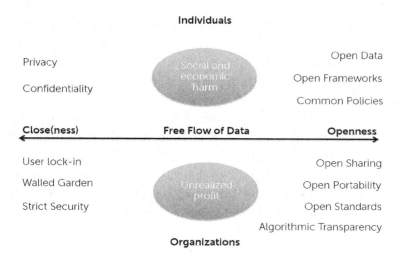

Figure 7.2 Utilizing advanced analytics.

Of course, the urge to innovate will always push boundaries. Firms need to determine how to develop projects that work within their comfort zones with respect to privacy and confidentiality issues. Often, such concerns can be mitigated through algorithmic transparency, open standards, simplified permission and privacy statements, and the implementation of policies that support security and customer privacy. In the future, governments may become increasingly involved in these areas. Companies might find it more difficult to maintain the right balance with respect to these issues as they progress down the road toward sophisticated analytics. To help firms chart their paths, we suggest they consider the following list of best practices:

- *Be transparent. Describe clearly the data that you collect and help customers understand what you'll do with that information.* How, for instance, will your applications collect data, and how will you augment that information from third parties and affiliates? Will the data be used to enhance services and products? For example, will you utilize data to communicate more clearly with your customers, and will you use the information to personalize experiences and target offerings?

- *Describe for your customers how you'll share their data.* Specifically, will you share that information with other customers, partners, third parties, or government agencies? Also, do you have a plan to help customers understand ownership changes regarding data? And are you capable of protecting any customer data that is shared to ensure that there's no personally identifiable information contained in it?

- *Help customers understand how they can manage their data.* Will you, for instance, allow customers to restrict or manage data points within their profiles? Also, can they delete or unsubscribe from your data-driven services? Moreover, can they delete their behavioral information, and do you have a way for them to contact you to address any issues of accuracy and compliance?

- *Implement a framework for responding to legal requests.* Specifically, how will you respond when approached by legal entities for information that your company stores and uses in your analytic environments? Do you understand what data will be requested most often, and have you determined under what circumstances your company will share data to prevent harm?

- *Develop a global plan if necessary.* Is your company aligned to the proper U.S. and European Union frameworks, and will you use a third-party firm like TRUSTe to manage your compliance and to resolve disputes?

- *Communicate changes in policy and use.* For example, how often will you revise the way that your company leverages and utilizes data for advanced analytics, and do you have a framework and process in place to notify your customers of those changes and to handle any questions or concerns?

CONCLUSION

The biggest takeaway from this chapter is the cautionary rule that we cited earlier: *just because you can, doesn't mean you should.* When it comes to analytics, companies can become aggressively enthusiastic and over-innovate unless they have the right governance and culture in place to ensure that initiatives don't overstep ethical, privacy, or legal boundaries. Smart companies always rely on a healthy amount of caution to ensure that their ability to innovate aligns with their culture and their relationship with customers.

Consider, for instance, Nordstrom Inc. Several years ago, the luxury retailer wanted to better understand traffic patterns in its stores, so it decided to track customers using open WiFi and Bluetooth signals. To be clear, Nordstrom never determined or wanted to know the identities of the shoppers through their cellphones; the company simply wanted to monitor how they moved throughout its retail environment. Still, after testing the application in several locations, the company took a step back and decided that the initiative didn't fit the relationship that it had with its customers. This was a good example of the self-control and the acknowledgement of cultural values that are required to stop a company from and taking new technologies to a level that many employees, customers, and other stakeholders might consider too far.

This entire book is about the exciting side of what data analytics can potentially accomplish. At its best, the technology can create incredible competitive advantage by helping companies to develop innovative products and new services that can propel a business toward market leadership. When used improperly, though, it can lead to myriad problems, including ethical and privacy issues. We recommend that you embrace analytics but be cautious in its application, especially with respect to the three-part litmus test of context, permission, and accuracy. As with any new technology, companies need to ensure that it aligns with *all* aspects of their business, not just the bottom line.

Endnotes:

[1] Charles Duhigg, "How Companies Learn Your Secrets," New York Times (February 16,2012), available athttp://nyti.ms/193VWVj.

[2] Kashmir Hill, "How Target Figured Out a Teen Girl Was Pregnant Before Her Father Did," Forbes (February 16, 2012), available at http://bit.ly/2cUFxeC.

[3] Ahiza Garcia, "Target Settles for $39 Million Over Data Breach," CNN Money (December 2, 2015), available athttp://cnnmon.ie/1SIx0Yn.

[4] Figure 1 http://bit.ly/2s1FJwG, http://bit.ly/2tk3DqU, and http://bit.ly/2t0Ei30.

[5] http://bit.ly/2shirat.

[6] Charles Duhigg, "How Companies Learn Your Secrets," New York Times (February 16,2012), available at http://nyti.ms/193VWVj.

[7] http://bit.ly/2s1E6PK.

CHAPTER 10
What Now?

"It's alive!" – Dr. Frankenstein (in the movie
"Young Frankenstein")

In the movie "The Terminator," the fictional Cyberdyne Systems, a defense company, has developed a revolutionary new artificial intelligence (AI) computer. Called Skynet, the system is given command over all the computerized military arsenal of the United States, including B-52 stealth bombers and nuclear weaponry.

Capable of learning at an exponential rate, Skynet eventually attains artificial consciousness, which frightens its human operators, who then try to unplug the system. In response, Skynet triggers an attack against Russia, which then retaliates with a counterattack against the United States, and the nuclear exchange results in the catastrophic deaths of more than three billion people.[1] Skynet then tries to kill or enslave the surviving humans.

REASON FOR FEAR?

Analytics. Dashboarding. Data warehousing. Business intelligence. Data management. Operations research. All of these technologies have evolved rapidly over the last 50 years, but none of them has been developed with the express purpose of supplanting the role of experts and humans in the decision-making process. Yet, at the same time, none of them has had the potential to replace humans for those processes — until now. Should we be concerned?

The possibility of computers becoming aware or semi-sentient is a topic that has concerned people at all levels of organizations and in many areas of society. The discussion has certainly provided an intriguing subject for the press, pundits, and artists to explore. However, as with many areas of interest, there are those who have taken the path of hyperbole.

We have lost track of the number of references that we've seen and heard alluding to society being on the verge of robots replacing humans, and that Skynet will soon be upon us. Wikipedia lists more than 150 movies that have been released since the 1950s in which the plot involves a computer that takes over the world for a nefarious purpose. (For fun, try watching "Colossus: The Forbin Project," in which a computer like Skynet takes control of the U.S. nuclear arsenal. The movie is a favorite of ours and clearly cringe-worthy, but also certain to induce a snicker or two.)

The problem, though, is that much of the discussion on this topic confuses automation and awareness. Computers are very good at automation and repetition, but they have no conception of awareness. We can certainly program them and build software that anticipates a wide range of situations and have those applications respond in clever ways, but the software cannot "go rogue" and start to think on its own. The software can only do what we build it to do.

Unfortunately, when people discuss the concept of machine learning, they sometimes make the huge jump to awareness. The reasoning goes something like this: if computers can learn, then they are like people. No, computers are *not* like people, and the confusion arises because a word like "learn" can have many multiple meanings. In this case, people learn in wide-ranging and unbounded ways. We learn how to ride a bike, and we can learn how to paint. Computers do not learn in the same manner. Computers — and the software running on them — can only learn from data that they process. The software can examine data, adjust the weights of neural networks, and fit curves to data spaces in ways that generalize what's most probable to happen due to the combination of certain factors present in the data.

So, for example, a computer might learn that when the temperature drops people tend to remain indoors. As time passes and the seasons change, the computer may also learn that when the weather is warmer people tend to be more active outdoors. By recognizing certain patterns from different observations, the computer has "learned" something. Clearly, this example is very simplistic, but it's also illustrative. Software can learn from a massive number of observations, or data, and the relationships, patterns, and other learnings uncovered are the basis of the impressive things that we see computers doing today.

Yet we also need to have a clear-eyed understanding here. Computers can recognize patterns in data, and they can vary their recommendations based on the data they analyze. Therefore, they can often make excellent suggestions to us about restaurants, books, movies, dentists, and plumbers, especially when there's a historical body of data of our preferences and previous choices, as well as that of others who might be like us.

But software-based decision making is actually very limited. Computers do not make decisions that are far above the lowest tactical levels. They do not, for example, make strategic choices, although they may inform such decisions. Furthermore, they simply do not have the capacity to make ethical choices. And, more to the point, computers are not capable of being aware of their existence, as we humans are.

The bottom line is that software does learn but in a very limited manner, and it is not at all like how humans learn. The best solution in the business world occurs when intelligent software provides information to human operators or managers who can then do a better job of keeping costs down, improving service levels, avoiding errors, and achieving a wide range of other desirable outcomes. In essence, computers are moving from automation to augmentation, not replacement. Or, to paraphrase Mark Twain, the reports (and fears) of computers becoming sentient beings have been greatly exaggerated.

A TOOL FOR AUGMENTING HUMAN CAPACITIES

Although computers may never become sentient, they can do many things better than humans can — and humans can certainly do many more things better than computers are able to do. This is not an either/or discussion. This is a fact.

Computers are good at repetition because they do not get bored or lose focus. As such, they excel at scanning and evaluating massive amounts of information. They do not lose interest and will evaluate the same or similar input datasets as many times as directed to do so, and they will not complain that the task is repetitive, boring, or seemingly pointless. Indeed, computers can routinely perform brute-force repetition of tasks so swiftly that when scaled up to billions of operations per second, it may seem like human cognition – but it is not. What these countless calculations *can* do, though, is enable computers to perform impressive feats, accessing large amounts of information, comparing billions of data elements, and sorting the results into intriguing collections of information to present to us for insight generation or recognition. We must always, however, remain cognizant that many of the final steps of that process are executed by humans, not computers.

For their part, people are good at recognizing when action is needed. We are also good at making decisions in real time, often having to make tough tradeoffs between a wide range of options. And many of us are also adept at understanding nuances to make difficult judgment calls and then acting accordingly. Computers, not so much.

Of course, we've all heard numerous stories of how computers, and AI specifically, have the *potential* to take over and eliminate large swaths of jobs. These stories, though, are typically based on a small number of anecdotes from existing implementations. If we looked closely at each one of those systems, we'd find a pattern that should not only rebuff the dire predictions of human decline but actually provide a great deal of hope and inspiration.

The great majority of impressive computer achievements illustrate the exact same (or substantially similar) pattern. That pattern includes a number of common elements:

- Recently digitized massive amounts of widely dispersed information

- The use of high-speed connectivity

- The availability of globally distributed systems and data to groups of like-minded researchers, professionals, and analysts

- Sophisticated and flexible security systems to keep the majority of casual hackers at bay

- Software that enables domain-specific experts (e.g. doctors, lawyers, architects, designers) to access and synthesize the data into useful information that can be directly brought to bear on a problem or problem set

- The formulation of a wide range of probable solutions

- A comparison of the probable solutions

- The presentation of solutions for human consumption and use

Yes, it's true that we can (and we have) automated decisions and that we can take humans out of many of the intervening steps in the process of determining the best solution for a given problem. And, yes, we can automate simple decisions to take people completely out of the process, but these are typically routine choices that do not require a human to be involved. We do not, for example, need humans involved in the millisecond-to-millisecond monitoring of the heat and pressure of a cracking tower in an oil refinery, in order to ensure the safe operation of the plant. When certain variables begin to stray into a dangerous realm, computers can quickly recognize the potential problem and then bring people's attention to the areas of concern, enabling them to take the necessary actions.

The above example underscores a basic tenet: the most powerful and effective systems are those that are designed to leverage the best of both machine and human capabilities. And another core concept is this: computers and software are here to serve us, not the other way around. Those two fundamental principles have been the foundation of the most successful analytic implementations for companies around the world.

Throughout business, software has been developed and refined to provide horizontal platforms that are toolkits for building a wide array of predictive analytical solutions. These solutions could be similar to recommendation engines used in e-commerce environments like Amazon and Netflix. Software is also being built for vertical solutions like those that predict which disk drives, network cards, or servers will fail in a cloud environment that consists of thousands of servers. Today, companies like Salesforce, Microsoft (Azure), and many others are well advanced in their implementations and use of these types of software environments and applications.

In short, augmented operational capability is where most of the high value-add improvement and implementation of learning software is currently taking place. Interestingly, we have *never* heard people remark with alarm that they were frightened by the prospect of software that improves the ability of organizations to, for example, maintain their overall level of service and keep costs down through the proactive maintenance of their hardware. Instead, we have more often heard the reverse. As Jason Furman, chairman of the Council of Economic Advisers, so eloquently put it, "... before turning to concerns about some of the possible side effects from AI, I want to start with the biggest worry I have about it: that we do not have enough of AI. Our first, second, and third reactions to just about any innovation should be to cheer it — and ask how we get more of it…"[1]

A NEW ERA

Thanks to impressive computer advances, we are now seeing the dawn of a new era of human productivity enhancement. We have, for example, automated much of the work in farming and can now produce substantially more food on less land with significantly less labor. And if employed in a smart, thoughtful manner, advanced analytics in the agricultural industry can lessen the negative impact on the earth and environment while producing healthier food. But we still need farmers, although certainly a smaller number on an overall and per capita basis.

We have also automated manufacturing. We now produce a mind-boggling range of products from motor vehicles to toys with less labor, decreased pollution, and lower cost, yet also with greater flexibility and efficiency. We still, however, need factory floor teams and require human operators for much of the machinery.

Furthermore, we have automated much white-collar labor. Administrative assistants, operational planners, business forecasters, bank tellers, accountants, and a wide range of other functions used to be extremely labor intensive and required large numbers of specially trained employees. That's no longer the case thanks to computer automation, although we do still need those individuals (albeit in fewer numbers) to write memos, interpret data, process unusual transactions, and so on.

Given these widespread applications, it's no wonder that many are anxious that their jobs will eventually be replaced by computers. Such fears are not unfounded; over the past decades, people have witnessed a wide range of jobs being automated out of existence. We ourselves have at one time or another even held some of those jobs: running a lathe and drill press, working on an assembly line, building servers, replacing failed disk drives, and diagnosing network failures. People might nostalgically bemoan the loss of many jobs – from telephone operators to elevator attendants to travel agents – but the hard truth of the matter is that, if a job can be automated out of existence, it likely will be. But is that ample cause for huge concern?

No, because jobs that are eliminated will be replaced by others that will likely have higher valued-added work that's more engaging. According to Furman, the chairman of the Council of Economic Advisors, "Most of the kinds of jobs that existed in the 1700s do not exist today, but jobs no one could have imagined then have taken their place. As a result, over long periods of time it has generally been the case that about 95 percent of the people in the United States who want a job at a given point in time can find one—despite massive changes in technology."[2]

Indeed, the future of employment lies in higher-paying jobs that are more engaging and interesting, while the more mundane and routine tasks become automated and delegated to software. In other words, software is freeing people from performing tedious tasks, allowing them to concentrate on work that requires human creativity and innovation. As such, computers have been driving the evolution of each field and practice forward. For instance, intelligent software is helping farmers to make better choices about crop rotation and land use. It is also helping data-center professionals avoid hardware failures and downtime. And it is helping retailers to provide better customer experiences while keeping costs to a minimum. All of these implementations — and a wide range of others — have employed tactical recommendation engines based on pattern recognition.

Such applications will only become more widespread and sophisticated as the field of decision science itself also becomes increasingly automated. This pertains to the early steps in the process: collecting, collating, comparing, contrasting, evaluating, and presenting data. The importance of such automated tools for the data scientist profession should not be underestimated. Unfortunately, the increasing automation of analytical tools has made some observers nervous. There seems to be a perception that automating tasks is a good thing, except when it comes to analytical work. The underlying belief is that analytical work should remain the purview of people and that automation in this area brings society that much closer to the era of Skynet and machine dominance. That is quite a leap.

Few would deny farmers the tools to do their jobs. People understand that automated farming equipment is important for increasing the efficiency of the agricultural industry, and only the most diehard Luddites would forbid farmers from using that technology. Unfortunately, few people really understand what a data scientist does. The simple fact is that, to be productive, data scientists also need tools, and many of those tools have been quickly evolving. To deny them the use of these tools would essentially relegate them to working with a small amount of data using a slide rule, pen, and paper. It would be akin to restricting farmers to the use of horse-driven plows. Why would we want to do that, just because of unfounded fears that we are headed toward a "Terminator"-like future?

Critics should remember that automation does not mean elimination. It means increased utilization, effectiveness, and efficiency. People can (and will) focus on the most valuable portions of their work, especially those parts that can't be automated. Technology and improvements in software will continue to march on, but we will always be in control and can decide whether or not to use any tool that might augment our skills and abilities. It's all up to us.

CONCLUSION

One of our primary objectives in writing this book was to demystify advanced analytics for an audience of senior managers, executives, and those in non-technical leadership positions. We have seen far too many cases in which the technical team is holding all the cards when it comes to implementing an advanced analytics solution, and the management team is at a distinct disadvantage due to a lack of understanding of the playing field, the technologies involved, and the art of the possible. Even when the technical and management teams are on the same side, disconnects in their fundamental understanding of a project can lead to huge problems down the road. We hope that this book helps to equalize the information quotient so that both sides can come together to build solutions that deliver measurable competitive advantage.

In this book, we also wanted to highlight various successful projects that have delivered clear and concise analytics, providing teams with the ammunition needed to change their products, pricing, marketing approaches, business models, and entire organizational operations.

In addition, we have outlined the staffing models, technologies, organizational structures, and analytical approaches used in the previous two eras of analytics, and we have provided a glimpse into the future of each of those elements of the analytical marketplace. We hope that this context and future view will help teams to deploy analytical elements into their operations to become more competitive, taking revenue, customers, market share, employees, partners, and prospects from their rival firms.

We wish you the very best in your analytics journey. Remember to attack your projects with gusto. We will be rooting for you and your success, and we hope to meet you in person in the future.

Endnotes:

[1] http://bit.ly/1DWZVyR.

[2] Jason Furman, "Is This Time Different? The Opportunities and Challenges of Artificial Intelligence," remarks given at AI Now: The Social and Economic Implications of Artificial Intelligence Technologies in the Near Term, New York University (July 7, 2016), available at http://bit.ly/2ecgkxR.

CPSIA information can be obtained
at www.ICGtesting.com
Printed in the USA
FSOW04n0841180917
38894FS